# THE FIVES TO FIFTEENS
# PARENTING PROGRAMME

# Leader's Guide

## Michael & Terri Quinn

# FAMILY CARING TRUST

First published 1986
by Veritas Family Resources.

Revised edition published 1989
by Family Caring Trust,
44 Rathfriland Road
Newry Co Down  BT34 1LD
Reprinted:  1992

Fully revised, and renamed
the Fives to Fifteens
Basic Parenting Programme,
January 1996.
Copyright © Family Caring Trust 1996
Reprinted Universities Press (Belfast) Ltd 2000
Reprinted Graham and Heslip Printers Ltd 2008

Illustrations:  John Byrne
Our thanks to 'Reality' magazine
for permission to reprint the passage
'Don't spoil me ...' in Appendix 2A

ISBN 1 872253 12 1

# CONTENTS

FAMILY CARING TRUST ACKNOWLEDGES

THE GENEROUS CONTRIBUTION OF

TOWARDS THE DEVELOPMENT AND PRODUCTION

OF THIS PROGRAMME

# HOW THIS PROGRAMME WORKS

MATERIALS
The materials for this programme are:

**This leader's guide** - containing all the information the group leader needs to set up the parenting programme and conduct each session of it. Because it is recommended that two people facilitate the course, two leader's guides are included in the boxed kit.

**The programme video** - providing a short input (about ten minutes or so) for each of the eight sessions of the course.

**Handbook for participants.** The handbook contains more detailed input and examples, table summaries of each chapter, and the various exercises for discussion, planning, etc. Parents usually pay for their own copy, and they are asked to read a short section of it before each session. There is not normally any other charge for the course, although that is something for leaders to decide.

**Pack of 25 Certificates** - may be presented at the end of a course.

**(Some extras - not included in kit)** The **Leader's tape** is helpful for running *any* of the Family Caring Trust courses, and may be purchased separately. The 25-minute **Introductory Video**, showing the effect of a course on two families, and made independently, is useful for an introductory session for *any* of the Trust's parenting courses. It may be purchased separately at nominal cost.

AN EIGHT SESSION COURSE
In this programme, there are eight sessions, held at weekly intervals. They correspond to the eight chapters of the parents' handbook. Each session lasts up to two hours and generally goes like this:

*1. Introduction to the session (1 min).*

*2. How everyone got on since the previous meeting (15-30 mins).*

*3. Getting in touch - a short exercise to help parents get in touch with the new topic at a personal level (5-10 mins).*

*4. Introducing the topic. The topic is introduced, based on the video-cassette (about 10 mins).*

*5. Case studies are discussed that help parents apply the input to typical family situations (about 10 mins).*

*6. Improving Your Skills - practising the new skill, usually in pairs (10-20 mins).*

*7. Planning. Parents are encouraged to make specific plans about how they will use the new skill during the week ahead (4-6 mins).*

*8. Relaxation and visualising. Followed by an **optional** Christian or Islamic reflection linked to the theme of the session (3-7 mins).*

*9. Summing up. A brief summary of the session is followed by some feedback from the group on how they found the session (5-10 mins).*

*10. Concluding remarks (1 min).*

The chapters of this book give detailed outlines for each session of the course. The remainder of this chapter may help you gain a better understanding of the above ten sections of each session.

## 1. INTRODUCTION (1 min.)

This is an opportunity to make everyone welcome, particularly anyone who, for whatever reason, may feel on the fringe of the group, for example single parents, people who see themselves in a lower social class, parents of children with a disability, people who feel shy, etc. It is also helpful to have a special word of welcome for anyone who missed the previous session.

The leader then explains simply and briefly what is going to happen during the session. When dealing with adults, it is best to involve them in what is happening as much as possible and not to have surprises.

## 2. HOW WE GOT ON SINCE LAST WEEK (15-30 mins)

Parents now have a chance to speak of their experiences with their children during the previous week, particularly in putting into practice what they have planned from the previous session. They need not confine themselves to the topic of the previous session, as they will often have other significant things to report. It is enough if they are speaking personally. This kind of personal sharing is *probably the most valuable part of the entire course.* It is disarming and freeing to hear a parent talk of little failures with children: that encourages others to trust the group as well. On the other hand, hearing of another parent's improvements is usually more convincing than anything a leader will say and is a strong incentive to parents to try out the ideas of the programme for themselves.

HOW THE PROGRAMME WORKS

The leader's role during this part of the session is to create an atmosphere of trust, to encourage efforts and improvements - and to use active listening to give members of the group a sense of being understood.

## 3. GETTING IN TOUCH WITH THE NEW TOPIC (5-10 mins)

Parents do a short exercise to help them get in touch with the new topic at a personal level and begin to apply it to themselves. This is usually done in pairs or threes, as people tend to feel more comfortable with that, particularly in the early stages of a course.

## 4. INTRODUCING THE TOPIC (about 10 mins)

Parents are expected to have read the short chapter from the parents' handbook in advance. Some parents will not have read the chapter because of poor reading skills, time-pressures, etc. In any case, the relevant section of the video, which is now shown, will be a reminder and a reinforcement of their reading. (If you do not have the video, an alternative input is provided in Appendix 1). Then parents can be encouraged to make any comments they wish or to apply the ideas to their own families. If they disagree with something, the leader's role is not to argue with them but to try to summarise or reflect back what they say in a genuine effort to understand (though not necessarily agree with) their point of view. There is no need to be defensive: the leader does not have to defend any of the ideas in this course and can be happy to see people thinking for themselves - that makes for a healthy group.

## 5. CASE STUDIES (about 10 mins)

The Case studies at the end of each chapter are now discussed in small groups. They offer parents an opportunity to apply the ideas they have just heard to typical family situations and thus deepen their understanding of the topic for that session. These case studies are also on audio tapes (supplied with earlier editions of this programme, and still available). If you wish, you may use the tapes at this point for variety, though some people find them a bit stilted. An advantage of using the case studies from the handbook is that the situations sound more natural when people speak in their own local accents - and an interesting side-effect is that parents who "act" the case studies often find it easier to enter into role-play situations later.

## 6. SKILL PRACTICE (20-25 mins)

The Case Studies are followed by an opportunity to practise the new skill, usually in pairs. Some people find this the most helpful part of the meeting as many of us learn better by *doing* than by discussion. Leaders are sometimes put off by the *explanation* of the skill practice, whereas the *experience* of it can be quite different.

The skill practice may be best planned in advance. On one or two occasions, for example, there is a short role-play, and some people take to role-play easily while others have considerable difficulty in entering into it. When volunteers are chosen in advance for this kind of exercise, it is important that people do not feel pressurised to do something they are not fairly comfortable with, and that they have a chance to "de-role" after any situation that may have stirred up strong feelings for them. That involves taking a little time to bring them back into the present, noticing their surroundings, and/or talking about the difference between how they have just acted and how they normally behave.

## 7. PLANNING FOR THE WEEK AHEAD. (4-6 mins)

This is an opportunity for everyone to plan how they will apply the ideas or skills at home. There are some suggestions at the end of each chapter. Parents often find it helps to have a minute or two of quiet to write down their plans before telling them to someone beside them. You can point out that they will have an opportunity to tell the group how they got on with their plans at the beginning of the following week's session. That can be an extra incentive to putting the ideas of the course into action.

## 8. RELAXATION AND REFLECTION. (4-10 mins)

Towards the end of each session, there is an opportunity to relax. It may help to dim lights and play a piece of reflective instrumental music softly in the background. Different methods of relaxation are introduced so that parents can find a method that suits them. They can then begin to use one of these methods, when necessary, to cope with stress in the home.

After the relaxation, parents are helped to visualise themselves relating differently to their children, perhaps foreseeing themselves using the new skill or carrying out the plans they have just made.

There follows an *optional* religious dimension - a few minutes of quiet reflection, linking the topic of the session with a short prayer and religious reflection (Christian or Islamic). The reflections for this course have proven so popular that groups not wishing to include a religious dimension are encouraged to adapt them in order to provide a similar experience. Most of them are not difficult to adapt.

## 9. SUMMING-UP. (5-10 mins)
This part of the session offers parents a chance to say how they are feeling, clarify what they have gained from the session, and learn from what others have gained. It can also offer a chance to express negative feelings like disappointment, confusion, etc. And it gives useful feedback to the leader. If there is little time, you can ask members of the group to be brief, even just to mention one *feeling* they have at that moment. If the feedback is negative, reflecting some confusion, for example, it will usually help to end on a positive note by encouraging people to share something they liked or gained from the session.

## 10. CONCLUDING REMARKS (1 min).
The leader encourages parents to read the new chapter in advance of the next meeting. Because of time pressures, poor reading skills, etc., some people will not manage to read the short chapter each week. The reading is not essential, but it is only about three pages, is simply written and is very much to be encouraged.

Arrangements can also be made at this stage about who will bring the snack for the next session.

## SOCIALISING AFTERWARDS
Parent education is greatly enhanced when it goes hand in hand with building community. Many of the exercises on the course facilitate community development, but providing a cup of tea or coffee is an additional help. It may help to start the *first* session with a cup of tea or coffee - that can be part of the welcome and allows for late comers. For

subsequent meetings, it is usually best to start punctually and have a simple snack *after* the session. That allows parents with baby-sitters to skip the snack and get home quickly if they wish to do so, but, more importantly, it gives the parents an opportunity to socialise and to talk about things that have risen during the meeting.

Responsibility for the snack can be rotated among the participants - which ties in well with the self-help ethos of the group.

# GETTING STARTED

A first glance at the Leader's Guide for a community programme can be over-awing, particularly if you have not *experienced* a course. This is not a complicated programme, however, and the purpose of this book is to lead you through it step by step.

## THE GROUP MIX

A group usually consists of ten to twelve parents. Participants learn a great deal from each other as trust builds up in the intimacy of a small group, so it may be important not to exceed this number. It helps to encourage *couples* to attend together - it is interesting that the vast majority of fathers who attend the courses come with their partners. (All-male groups have also been quite successful - people tend to feel more comfortable when they are not the only one of their kind - the only man in a group, the only black person, the only parent of teenagers, the only lone parent, the only parent of a child with a disability...)

There is great value in mixing groups. With the best of intentions, you may want to arrange separate groups exclusively for parents of children with a disability, for lone parents, etc. (and special interest groups may *need* to meet, perhaps monthly, to discuss situations that are unique to them). But we must be careful not to marginalise people further by arranging their entire lives around their special need, interest or disability. It has been encouraging to see how parents from different social backgrounds, and with children from different age groups, have mixed well and bonded together. This may need to be borne in mind particularly in resisting pressure to form groups exclusively for "problem" parents. All parents have problems, but, if the people in your group are *all* parents referred to you by social services, it may be more difficult to break unhelpful parenting habits - and you also risk sabotaging the entire parenting initiative in your community when it appears to be only for people with serious problems.

Another advantage in mixing groups is that it is sometimes harder for parents to make changes if they know each other too well before the course. There are many exceptions to this guideline, however - see what you find works for yourself.

## FINDING THE PARTICIPANTS

People tend to respond best to a friend's invitation, an invitation from a school principal or parent-teacher organisation, or from an existing community or church group with which they identify. Beware of putting pressure on people: parents need to come freely and willingly.

A sample letter from a school principal has been included at the end of this book. It has been helpful in encouraging many parents of schoolchildren to attend parenting courses. In some areas, the response to an invitation through the school has been almost nil; in other areas, the letter has had a fifty five percent response. It can be adapted as you wish in targeting community or other groups.

Some schools have found another successful way of recruiting parents - bringing them together for a parent-teacher meeting or an induction meeting for parents of first year schoolchildren at either primary or secondary school, and devoting about thirty minutes to the idea of support for parenting. When the twenty five minute introductory video (see page 4 for details) is shown at this meeting, many of those present tend to sign up for a course. It may be important to have forms available so that parents can sign up for courses after the meeting.

## WHERE COURSES ARE RUN

Many leaders of groups have commented on the breaking down of social barriers and the growth in community spirit that occurs during a course - and research shows that people learn better when this sense of community is present. But it appears that a better bond is usually built and a greater community spirit created when a group meets in someone's home rather than in a school, church or institutional building. Not every home is suitable - much depends on the ages of the children and how distractions are coped with. But that feedback is worth considering.

Courses have also been run in community centres, parish halls, school libraries, staff-rooms, even classrooms. For obvious reasons, a classroom is not ideal - but we do not always have an ideal setting.

# GETTING STARTED

Whenever possible, meetings need to be held in comfortable, pleasant surroundings.

## KEEPING ATTENDANCE UP.

No course is going to suit everyone. It is reasonable to expect a fall-off of one or two people after the first one or two sessions, although there is often no fall-off at all. Sometimes, a parent misses a meeting and thinks that too much ground has been lost. Other parents may be a little fearful and may need encouragement. If parents do miss a meeting, it may be a good idea for the leader to phone or call to say how much they were missed and to enquire about them, but it is obviously not helpful to spend time chasing up people who are missing consistently or who are just not interested in continuing.

## HOW OFTEN TO MEET.

There are so many relatively new skills taught on the course that parents sometimes react to meeting weekly. A week does not seem to give them enough time to integrate the ideas and practise the skills. There is something in these parents' objections. When leaders experimented with meeting at longer intervals, however, *less* seemed to happen between sessions and parents invariably requested weekly meetings again. The impetus of regular meetings seems to be a valuable part of the learning process.

## FINDING AND TRAINING LEADERS

The model of community development underlying this course is not a western one but one from the "third world" (what we prefer to call the "majority world"). It requires a deeply respectful approach that is not satisfied with merely *enriching* or *supporting* people; rather, it believes in people's potential to emerge as leaders within their own communities. People are seen as having something to *offer* rather than as needing to be "helped." It can sometimes be difficult for professional people to appreciate this emphasis if they have been trained to provide remedial care for families.

Leaders of this parenting course do not need professional qualifications or a high level of education. They are not expected to be "experts" or to give any input, for the input comes from the video and form the books. Most leaders are ordinary parents, though it's not even essential that they be parents - many excellent courses have been run by people who are not in a parenting role. Perhaps the most important qualification a leader can have is to be a good listener - with genuine respect for parents' experience, for their differences, and for their natural instinctive wisdom. Leaders will be most convincing when they have a belief in the principles of the programme and a willingness to keep applying the new skills both in the group and in their own relationships.

We believe that everyone is a potential leader, but the experience of repeated criticism and put downs, particularly in childhood, can make it difficult for many of us to claim that natural leadership which is our right. It is our experience, however, after ten years of monitoring this programme, that there tend to be one or two people with a certain readiness for taking leadership in most groups - they may stand out because of their enthusiasm and commitment to practising the skills between sessions, or because of their respect for others. At the end of the course, you might ask them *individually* (please do not ask for "Any volunteers") to assist you in running a new course. You may need to deal with people's fears about "leadership," helping them to see that this has nothing to do with the old style of authoritarian leadership - that leadership is simply about making a difference in people's lives. Obviously, new people will need to become familiar with the programme materials, especially the Leader's Guide. There is a great deal of learning in the *experience* of leading a group with the help of the leader's guide. As the new course progresses, you can begin to take a back seat as the assistant leader grows in confidence and is able increasingly to take over the running of the session. Experience also indicates that there is a lot to be said for having *two* leaders in each group - many people who would otherwise have felt too shy have only consented to leading a group provided there would be this sharing of leadership and mutual support.

One of the best ways to acquire the skills taught on this programme is to lead a group. Then, after some time, leaders can begin to move on to other community work. Many of them will have grown so much in confidence and in their use of group skills that they are able to serve their communities in a variety of different ways.

# GETTING STARTED

## KNOWING YOUR LIMITATIONS

Some parents will come on the courses with problems that require *special* expertise or counselling. One parent may need bereavement counselling before being able to respond effectively to her children; another may need support in dealing with drugs or alcohol in the family; another may need marriage counselling - or counselling around having been sexually abused as a child. It is important that group leaders recognise their limitations and do not attempt to deal with these problems themselves. You are encouraged to draw up a list of local agencies and telephone numbers so that you are in a position to put someone in touch with whatever expertise and support they need.

## ONGOING SUPPORT FOR LEADERS

Some leaders seem to emerge naturally in a community, but most leaders are "grown." We have already seen how this can begin to happen - and the process is helped when they take a few minutes after sessions to evaluate their own performance, talk out any difficulties that may have arisen, and note improvements. It is also common for leaders of different courses to contact each other between sessions in order to talk out difficulties and support each other.

Some ongoing support from other leaders would seem to be essential. They seem to need an opportunity to meet with others working in similar fields, to hear each other's experience, and to talk about their discoveries, difficulties, breakthroughs, plans, etc. All the better if some further enrichment, skills training and awareness raising can also be provided.

This kind of support is increasingly being provided, sometimes on a monthly basis, sometimes only one or twice a year, by local networks of health visitors or schools, by church family ministry departments, and by organisations like Barnardos. Increasingly, these voluntary groups are co-operating with and being supported by statutory services - health education authorities, social services, community education, psychological services, etc. Such supportive networking is to be encouraged for it makes the entire parenting initiative much more community based and effective.

GETTING INTO ACTION

Let's look then at how to get the programme established in your community, organisation, church or school. Here is one possible plan of action, though you may prefer to choose only *some* elements from it.

1. Find a comfortable place to hold the meetings (perhaps your own home!)
2. Set a date.
3. Invite some friends to experience the course.
4. Run the course for eight consecutive weeks - or you may like to share or revolve the leadership, letting different people use the leader's guide for successive sessions.
5. For the next course, choose one or two "assistants" from among the participants and give them the programme materials to study.
6. Run a second course, allowing your assistant(s) to take increasing responsibility for leading it.
7. Evaluate, and plan for your community/ organisation/ church/ school.
8. Eventually appoint a co-ordinator.

# THE LEADER'S ROLE

The previous chapters give some indication of what is expected of a group leader. Let's look at that in more detail now.

One of the most important things a leader can do is create a friendly, caring atmosphere. Your welcome, the cup of tea or coffee, your ongoing concern for and interest in the parents can do a great deal to help them relax and to build a sense of community and caring in the group.

## NOT AS AN EXPERT

During this course it does not help to act as an expert or teacher, nor to encourage parents to look to you for answers. They can find some answers in the video, in the parent's book, and in the experience of the other members of the group. Basically, however, parents need to be encouraged to see that they are different, that other people's answers may not work for them, that they have to find their *own* answers. So you might answer their questions with:

"What do you think yourself?" "What does the book say about that?" or "Has anyone else any experience of this?"

At times, this will be hard to do, especially when parents ask questions around something you feel strongly about, like "What do you think about punishing children?" Providing answers, even good answers, to these questions, may not be helpful: instead of *empowering* parents, you may be undermining their confidence, becoming yet another "expert" for them to look up to, and making it difficult for them to believe in their own ability to work out appropriate solutions with the support of the group.

Even if members of the group disagree or get stuck in an argument, the leader is best not to come up with a "solution" but to help them to move on. You might say something like: "I'm always surprised at how different things work for different people. I wonder though if we can move on now and come back to this point later..."

## USING THE SAME SKILLS AS THE PARENTS

Many leaders find that the skills they require are precisely the same skills as are taught on this programme - encouragement, listening, "I" messages, etc. Anyone in a leadership position will tend to find these skills useful in everyday life - parents, teachers, managers, ministers, group leaders...

One of the most important things the leader can do is encourage. It may be up to you to remind a discouraged member of the group: "Well, I see you feel discouraged about that, but how does the way you handle it now compare with the way you *used* to handle it?" Keep listening for efforts, strengths and improvements, and reflect them back to the parents in a sincere, honest way.

That brings us to a vital leadership skill - listening. Your success in leading the group will depend much more on how you listen than on how you talk. Try to give everyone a sense of being understood, even if they are attacking basic elements of the course. If someone thinks that "active listening" is merely opting out of effective discipline, for example, it will not help to argue; see if you can grasp what they are saying and check if you have understood that correctly. In that way you are neither agreeing nor disagreeing, but you are respecting the person who is objecting. Trust the process. Members of the group who have a sense of being listened to can feel free to change and grow at their own pace.

Another great quality you can bring to the group is your honesty about your *own* family. You can help to build up the vital trust level in the group by making a contribution during the "How we got on" section at the beginning of a session. When you let people hear about your difficulties and your failures as well as your successes, that will often give them permission to open up in turn and risk talking about their own family situations. Equally, when a group seems to be getting bogged down in discussion of ideas, it can help to talk about yourself and your family in relation to the topic being discussed. That helps to draw people away from theory and begin to apply the ideas to themselves. But beware of using this as a licence for over-talking. Your main role is to lead by listening and encouraging.

## DEALING WITH OVER-TALKATIVE PEOPLE.

Sometimes a parent will tend to hog the meeting. If this is happening, it is no harm to highlight again, at the beginning of a session, the relevant groundrule from the back of the parents' handbook - encouraging others to talk and not talking a second time until the others have had a chance to speak. Chronic talkers may ignore this, however, so another possibility is to interrupt them with something like:

"Do you mind if I cut in on you here, Margaret? I'm keeping an eye on my watch and I'm anxious to get through the programme for this session, so we'll need to move on, but maybe we could talk about this point over the cup of tea afterwards."

Better still, you might use the group itself to restore order and to keep to the schedule. You can cut in on someone and say:

"I'm sorry to interrupt you, Joe, but maybe we could ask the group if they want to deal now with this point you have brought up - or would they prefer to move on to the next part of our programme for the session?" Involving other members of the group often helps to control the over-talkative one, for example when you wait for a pause for breath and nip in with: "Would you like to comment on that, Omar?" or, "What do you think of that, Phil" or, "Why do you think that is so difficult for parents, Liz?" (But it is important not to hop onto someone who finds it difficult to talk in the group.)

One way to draw timid people into the group, and at the same time control people who tend to over-talk, is to take the talker aside before or after the meeting and ask for help in drawing the other person out. Giving that responsibility can help both of them.

THE NEED FOR FLEXIBILITY.
Throughout this Leader's Guide there is a suggested script, giving the actual words which the leader can use to introduce a section or to link sections together. This can be a useful aid to people who are inexperienced in facilitating groups, but the script need only be used in so far as it is helpful. Please feel free to ignore it. You may be able to explain things more simply in your own words.

Finally, it is important not to be rigid. Just try to be present to the members of the group and allow them all to apply what suits themselves. When you are flexible and adaptable - open to different approaches and different experience - the entire group will tend to make better progress. There are no *rules* for parenting, just guidelines. And guidelines don't apply always or in the same way to everyone.

# THE LEADER'S ROLE

Be flexible, too, in the use of group work - it depends so much on the number of people in your group, on their backgrounds and experience. Someone who feels shy, for example, may be frightened of speaking in a group of ten people but happy to chat away in twos or threes. Moreover, when you are trying to keep an eye on the clock, you may find it easier to interrupt two or three small groups than to cut in on a single group. At the same time, something is missing when people are not exposed to the wider group. So see if you can strike a balance. Use your own judgement rather than follow the instructions in this leader's guide too rigidly. This applies particularly after running the course once or twice. As you grow in confidence, you may discover more effective ways of helping parents to learn. We are always pleased to hear from group leaders about their experience - both their difficulties and their breakthroughs - in order to share it in our newsletter or incorporate it into future editions.

## A WAY OF LIFE RATHER THAN A SET OF SKILLS

Finally, an added bonus. What often becomes apparent to people is that the skills taught in the parenting programmes are much more than skills. They challenge us to adopt an entire way of life founded on respect for those around us. To become an encouraging person. To become a better listener. To consult more using the skills for managing problems. To speak directly to the person with whom we have tension rather than complaining about them to others. To use "I" messages. To delegate responsibilities and show increasing trust in people's capabilities. These skills, then, are not a set of techniques for getting children or anyone else to do things for us. They are more a set of *attitudes*. And these attitudes begin to infuse all our relationships.

# AN INTRODUCTORY SESSION?

**CHECKLIST: Materials**

Leader's Guide.

Handbooks (one per person, including leaders)

Pencils or pens (preferably pencils)

Video player and cassette - pre-set.

Simple snack - biscuits and tea or coffee.

Music cassette & player (for relaxation)

**CHECKLIST: Before session begins**

Set videocassette at correct position and volume.

Make pencils available, for example on floor at one side.

If necessary, delegate someone to take responsibility for snack.

Set music cassette at correct position.

You may not wish to add an extra session to a course which already makes considerable demands on your time, but some leaders like to hold a preliminary or introductory information session to explain about the course and the need for it, and to deal with any questions parents may have. This can help to get things off to a good start and parents will tend to come to the first session proper in a more relaxed and more receptive frame of mind. During an introductory session, any of the following things can be done (though not necessarily all of them, nor in this order):

•   The 25-minute 'introductory video' can be shown (see page 5).

•   One or two parents, preferably a man and a woman, might be invited to speak briefly about their personal experience of attending a course, giving their reasons for attending (and possibly their reluctance to attend), and what they gained from it.

•   Handbooks can be distributed - and possibly money collected.

•   Some introductory exercises can be done from the outline for Session One, including an icebreaker, discussion of the Groundrules/ Agreements from the back of the parents' handbook, and marking and discussion of the 'Rights' page at the beginning of the book. (You will need to modify Session One accordingly.)

•   The session might end with music and a relaxation exercise, with encouragement to practise the relaxation again at home. Something like:

**I'll put on some background music to help you relax, and you're asked to sit comfortably, and put both feet on the ground so that**

**you're more grounded - close your eyes if that helps, and breathe more deeply and slowly...** (30 secs) **Imagine yourself now in a place you love, near the mountains or sea or trees or flowers...** (30 secs) **Relax and enjoy the scene all around you...** (30 secs) **Notice the sounds...** (30 secs) **Notice smells now, of sea or flowers or whatever...** (30 secs) **Lie down, in your imagination, and feel the breeze or the sun on your face...** (30 secs) **Now, slowly come back to the room...** (30 secs) **When you're stressed, it may help to do an exercise like this for a few minutes. Parents often feel lighter and better after it.**

• For homework they can be asked to read Chapter 1 and to observe - can they see the ideas of Chapter 1 applying in their own family?

It may help to negotiate with the group about finance. Decide first whether your work is voluntary, or have you decided to make a charge for your services? Will you have a fixed charge to cover the cost of their book and snacks, or would they prefer to make a weekly contribution instead? Or would they like to take turns in providing the snack themselves? In keeping with the respectful approach and the self-help nature of the group, it helps to consult them about these decisions.

Some of those attending an information meeting may ask what you *do* during the course. While it is difficult to describe the *experience* of a parenting course, it helps to be as upfront as possible - *we start with an icebreaker to help us get to know each other better, we watch a short section of video and talk about it with someone sitting beside us, we do short exercises like - tick any of the following behaviours you find hard to cope with in any of your children - or here's a situation; how would you cope with it? And each week we plan something to try out a new approach with one of our children...*

The beginning of a course is also a good time for parents to get the backing of their own partners, parents, and/or extended family. If only one parent is taking the course, invite them to ask their partner, if they have one, for active support *before* they begin, so that what they are trying to do is not undermined. For those families where only one parent can attend, the video might be sent home for the spouse/ partner, and even grandparents, to watch, - another way of getting them behind the person taking the programme. It has often been found helpful, too, to have the other adults who live in the home read the parents' handbook.

# SESSION ONE

**CHECKLIST: Materials**

Your leader's guide.

Handbooks (one per person - if they do not already have them)

Pencils or pens (preferably pencils).

Slips of paper, one per threesome (write or photocopy from "Introduction").

Video player and cassette - pre-set.

Snack - if group is not bringing it.

Reading lamp or candle/matches, music cassette and player, for relaxation exercise (and for optional reflection).

Audiotape for session 1 (not included in kit), if you prefer to use it instead of case studies.

**CHECKLIST: Before session begins**

Set videocassette at correct position and volume.

Make pencils available, for example on floor at one side.

If necessary, delegate someone to take responsibility for snack.

Set music cassette at correct position and volume.

Reading light plugged in and ready.

If you will be using a section of the Appendix, you may like to mark it with a bookmark or paper clip.

Before the first meeting it helps to arrange the chairs in an informal, circular fashion with no classroom overtones. Go through the checklist to make sure you have everything you need for the session. Pencils are preferable to pens, because parents can decide later to rub out the ticks they have made if they wish.

The first meeting follows a slightly different format to the other sessions, as people will first need to be introduced to each other and to the general format of the programme (unless this has happened at an introductory session).

1. INTRODUCTION. (10-12 mins)

Make everyone welcome, and explain the aim of the course. Something like:

**I'd like to start by thanking you for coming this (evening), for caring enough about your children to want to improve as parents, and for your generosity in giving up your time to do that. Anyone who feels a bit shy is especially welcome because you've had the**

courage to come along in spite of your feelings. But I think you'll find the course enjoyable - most people do.

This is a programme for ordinary parents, although the fact that you've decided to give up so much of your time to do the course is a sign that you've not just ordinary - you have a desire to be better parents and you're prepared to do something about it.

The purpose of the course is to improve the way we get along with our children, to help us to communicate better with them and to discipline them more effectively. I think you'll find it practical - it certainly won't be just theory - and there'll be plenty of opportunities to apply the ideas at home and in the group. The aim is to become more effective as parents and to encourage a growing sense of responsibility and co-operation in our children.

I want to make it clear right from the beginning that I'm not here to give you advice on parenting. My job is to play the video, move you through the different sections of the session, and help you come up with your *own* solutions. No one knows your children as well as you do, and each one of you is different - your family background is different, your children are different. So, obviously, we need different approaches - there isn't just one way to bring up children.

There is a script here in this leader's guide, and I'm following it in what I say, apart from a few personal examples. So the input in this course will come from the video and from the books - not from me, and you can apply it in any way you like. I want you to feel free to disagree with anything that wouldn't suit your family.

We'll start by getting to know each other. I know that some people hate going around the circle and saying their names and so on, so it might be more enjoyable and relaxed if we form into small groups of three or four people. I'd like you all to get to know each other, so it's probably best to choose people whom you don't know, or at least people whom you don't know *well*. I have some questions here that we can chat about to begin to get to know each other. I would ask you to make sure that everyone gets an opportunity to speak about each of the questions - you could take them one at a time and go around your small group. Perhaps we'll take five minutes on that...

It may help to read aloud what is written on the slip of paper. Then give out the slips, one per threesome, with the questions written on them. You may need to help to form groups, with three people in each group (and certainly not more than four, for that can be scary for some parents). This exercise helps to break the ice and get people to relax, and it usually changes the atmosphere quite a bit. The questions are:

---

*Please make sure each person in your group gets a chance to talk about a question before moving on to the next question each time.*

**What is your name and where do you come from originally?**

**How many children do you have, and what stages are they at?**

**What fears do you have about what will happen on this course?**

**What made you want to come, and what would you like to gain?**

---

After this chat, you may like to ask for a handshow as you ask:

**How many parents have at least one child 5 or under?**

**How many parents have a child aged 6, 7 or 8?**

**How many parents have a child aged 9, 10, or 11?**

**How many parents have a child aged 12, 13, or 14?**

**And how many parents have a child aged 15 or over?**

It may help to point out to parents of teenagers that this is a *general* parenting programme with examples from *various* age groups, and that parents of teenagers are encouraged to do it first but often follow up with the 'Parenting Teenagers' Programme within a year or so.

2. HOW MEETINGS ARE RUN. (5 mins)

Explain how the sessions work. Something like this:

**Well, as you probably know, we'll have eight weekly meetings, each lasting up to two hours. We start each meeting by talking about how we got on with our plans from the previous meeting - that's usually quite interesting. Then we get into the topic by doing a "Getting in Touch" exercise. Next, we take about 10 minutes to watch a video and talk about it. We then look at some family situations and talk about how we might handle them, and we can also practise some situations in twos or threes. Before the end of each session, we take a few minutes to plan what we're going to do in the**

**week ahead, and then we relax and wind down with music. We end by giving anyone who likes a chance to comment or say what's going on for them.**

**I'll give out the books now. Could you start by turning to the back of the parent's book and looking at the Groundrules or Agreements...? Would you like to take turns in reading aloud one at a time? - But anyone who doesn't want to read just say "Pass."**

Distribute the books, if they have not already been distributed. If you wish, you can read the Agreements aloud or allow people to read them silently, but one advantage of taking turns is that it may alert you that some of the group have poor reading skills - you can then read exercises aloud for the rest of the course rather than assume people can read.

**Are you all happy to agree these Groundrules, or is there anything else that would help you to feel safer or more comfortable in the group?**

If you think some Agreements are being overlooked during the course, it may help to come back to this page at the beginning of a later session and highlight one or two points again.


3. GETTING IN TOUCH WITH THE NEW TOPIC (5-10 mins)
We can begin this section by asking everyone to take a few minutes to do the "Getting in touch" exercise at the end of Chapter One.

**We're ready now to move on to the first topic, which is children's misbehaviour. By misbehaviour we mean anything which children do that doesn't respect themselves or respect you or respect others. If you open your books at the "Getting in touch" section at the end of Chapter One, you could take a few minutes to tick any misbehaviours in that list that tend to bother you in your own family. Some parents put the first letter of their child's name beside the misbehaviour - whatever you like...**

As with all exercises in future, read this section aloud if you suspect some parents have poor reading skills.

**You might also underline one area where you'd like to be more effective... (1 min)**

**Feel free now to talk together in twos or threes, especially about the behaviour you'd like to deal with and what you normally do about it - you see the questions there?** (2 mins)

**Well, what's the one thing you'd like to be more effective in dealing with...?**

It is good to hear a number of parents *naming* these behaviours - parents are thus making it safe for each other to admit that all is not perfect in their families. The sense of solidarity that flows from this kind of sharing is an important part of what makes the group effective.

## 4. INTRODUCING THE TOPIC (about 10 mins)

The videocassette for Session 1 may now be played. (When the video is not available, you may use the alternative introduction to the topic from Appendix 1 at the back of this Guide.)

After watching the video, encourage the participants to talk in pairs for a minute or so about their reaction to it (the talking is best done in pairs and not in the full group for the first few sessions, so that people who feel shy don't feel under threat). After a minute or so:

**Would anyone like to make a comment about the video, or disagree with anything, or say how these ideas might apply in your family...?**

If people react, or are critical of the ideas, please respect their right to disagree, and do not argue or defend the ideas. You might say something like: **"Yes, some people don't find these ideas helpful - we're all different and we're going to find that different things will help different people. So throughout this course, I want you to feel perfectly free to ignore whatever you don't find helpful."** Or you might say, **"Thanks for saying that. My job is not to defend any of the ideas on this course. The group is meant to help you make your *own* decisions, and I feel encouraged that you already feel free to state your own opinions. I can see it's going to be a healthy group."**

Then continue with the Case Studies.

## 5. CASE STUDIES (about 10 mins)

**You can form into groups of three now, look at the Case Studies at the end of Chapter 1, and take a few minutes on each situation...**

As we saw above, it is less threatening to work in small groups for the first few sessions, but some leaders find the parents enjoy taking parts and reading the situations aloud. That creates a laugh and tends to make the situations more real for them. If you are asked questions, help people to make their own decisions by turning back the question - even if their choices are different to what you would choose. Discussing the case studies will often widen the parents' horizons and help them see that there is not just one way to handle a situation. These case studies are also on audio tapes (supplied with earlier editions of this programme, and still available). You may like to use the tapes for this section because of the variety they add to a session, though some people find them a bit stilted. An advantage to using the case studies from the handbook is that people are speaking in their own local accents - and an interesting side-effect is that they find it easier to enter into role-play situations later.

## 6. SKILL PRACTICE (20-25 mins)

The next section can be introduced something like this:

**Well, we've been looking this (evening) at ways in which we can avoid taking the bait, ways of breaking unhelpful habits of parenting that we may have been using for years. But how do we begin to change? We're told there are three steps in making a change, and that the first step is to become *aware*. So let's try something to make us aware of some of the unhelpful habits we have that we may have picked up from our own parents or guardians. Perhaps we find ourselves using the same tone of voice or the exact some words that our parents used. Or some of us *react* against the way we were brought up by doing the *opposite* to what our parents did... Both are unthinking patterns, so it can be useful to stand back from it all and ask ourselves: "Is this how we *want* to treat our children?"**

**The suggestion, then, is that you form pairs and talk for a few minutes about the ways in which your own parents or guardians brought you up, and then ask yourself: "What effect does that have on me today in *my* approach to my children?" If one of you would like to talk first in each pair, I'll give you a signal after two minutes and the other person can then take *their* turn.**

Occasionally, this exercise may touch into painful memories, so do not allow it to continue for longer than two minutes each way, even though parents may have much more to say. If there is time, ask:

**Well, any comments on that or what did you find...? What kind of things did your parents say that you find yourself saying? Anyone find that they're doing the opposite to what their parents did - maybe giving *too* much freedom or something?**

## 7. PLANNING FOR THE WEEK AHEAD. (4-6 mins)

This is an opportunity for everyone to plan how they will apply the ideas from Session One over the next week.

**There are three stages to making a change and we've just seen that the first stage is awareness. The second stage is to make a *specific* and *small* plan, preferably written down - so you may like to take a few minutes now on the "Planning" section at the end of chapter 1, and make a note of your plan on the line at the bottom. I'd remind you not to aim too high - just to settle for a little at a time. All we're trying to do in this first session is to begin to break our normal pattern, to unhook, not to take the bait....**

It may help to read this section aloud. Then after two or three minutes, you can continue:

**You can talk in pairs about your plans now and tell each other what you intend to do - telling someone what you've planned usually helps to make it happen! Couples may prefer to plan together.**

After a further 2-3 minutes you might say:

**You may be wondering what the third stage of making a change is. And it's pretty obvious - practise, practise, practise. A new approach will feel awkward and unnatural at the beginning, and you may feel discouraged. That's normal for any new skill - riding a bike or learning to type or whatever. But it quickly becomes second nature. So I look forward to hearing next week how you get on.**

## 8. RELAXATION (AND OPTIONAL REFLECTION) 4-10 mins.

This next section offers parents a time of calm towards the end of a session. They have an opportunity to relax and to imagine or foresee themselves putting into action some of the ideas from the session.

# SESSION ONE

It may help to change the atmosphere by dimming the lights, lighting a reading light or candle, and playing appropriate music softly in the background. (The music may also be helpful for people who are uncomfortable with silence.)

**We're coming to the end of the session now, so we'll have a quietening down time and a short reflection. I'll put on some background music to help you relax, and you're asked to sit comfortably, perhaps keep your back straight, and put both feet on the ground so that you're more grounded - close your eyes if that helps, and breathe more deeply and slowly...**

After half a minute, it may help their concentration to remind them:
**Just relax, breathing deeply and slowly...**

After a further 30 seconds, lower the music a little and continue:
**That's something you might consider doing when you feel stressed - just, if possible, to sit down for a few minutes, and relax by breathing in and out more deeply. Apparently that's one way to cope with stress in our lives. Each week we'll try different ways of relaxing so you'll find something that suits you.**

Read the following slowly, pausing for a little while each time you come to continuous dots:

**In this session, we've been looking at ways of taking a new and different approach with our children. One way to do that is to pay *good* attention to them when they're *not* expecting it. So, perhaps keeping your eyes shut, let's imagine that for a moment.**

**Imagine a time during the coming week when you're tempted to catch up on something you want to do and then you stop and think "No, I'll try a little bit of positive parenting - I'm going to *enjoy* one of my children, just for these few minutes." Decide which child it is - can you see the face...? Relax, now, and imagine yourself slowing down and taking time to sit and listen or play a game or have a chat with that child... (brief pause.) Don't talk much - just see yourself being relaxed and present and making the time... (pause) Look at your son or daughter now and notice how pleased they are to have your full attention... (pause). And when you're ready, you can come back slowly to the room we're in and open your eyes and relax... (pause).**

## SESSION ONE

**Well done! What you have just done didn't take long, but when you give positive attention like that, you'll see the benefits in the weeks and months to come...**

Let the music fade out gradually - do not switch it off abruptly. If you are using the optional religious dimension, however, you can let the music continue to play as you read the reflection. The text for the reflections is at the back of this book in appendix 2A (Christian) or 2B (Islamic). This is an optional section for church groups, etc., but it is so popular that groups not wanting a religious dimension are encouraged to adapt it and reflect along similar lines.

### 9. SUMMING UP. (5-10 mins)

It is helpful to take a short time at the end of a session to allow parents to make any comments, to express their thoughts or feelings, to tell what they plan to do, to appreciate what they have gained or to disagree with something. It is also a useful way of checking out what has been gained and of clarifying a point that may have been misunderstood. This part of the meeting can be introduced something like this:

**To finish our meeting, I just want to give you a few minutes to say how you're feeling now about this course. Feel free to say what you plan to do next week - or which part of the session you weren't so happy about, or what you found helpful... Whatever you need to say...**

If there is time, it may help instead to ask:

**Would you like to say in *one* word how you're feeling now at the end of this session - confused, relaxed, upset, hopeful, whatever...**

### 10. CONCLUDING REMARKS (1 min).

**Some of you may feel that this was quite a negative topic for our first session, but, if awareness is the first step in making a change, maybe we *needed* to start by becoming aware of unhelpful and ineffective habits of parenting we may have. You'll find next week's topic much more positive. It's about developing a sense of responsibility in children, so you're asked to have Chapter 2 read in advance. We tend to get more out of a session when we've read the chapter in advance.**

**I'd also like this to become *your* group, so a different person takes responsibility each week for the snack. By "snack" I mean a packet**

31

of biscuits and a pint of milk. If you prepare an elaborate snack, that puts pressure on others to do the same. So just something simple. Could we have a volunteer for that for next week...?

One final thing. If you find that you can't get here next week because of some emergency, maybe you'd ring and let us know and keep in touch. So I look forward to meeting you again next week and to hearing how you get on with a new approach. And thank you for your trust in coming along today.

AFTER THE MEETING.

After each meeting it helps to do a brief evaluation with your co-leader, if you have one, or personally. You might ask yourselves, for example: Did we talk too much? Did we answer questions or toss them back to the group? Are group members beginning to look to themselves for answers or do they see us as the "experts"? Did any problems arise? What can we do about that? Who needs encouragement? What will we change the next time?

It may help to talk with other leaders of other groups between sessions, even just to share difficulties and successes.

*Remember to turn questions back!*

# SESSION TWO

**CHECKLIST: Materials**
Your leader's guide.
Your parents' handbook
Pencils or pens (preferably pencils).
Newsprint (blank), adhesive and fibre-tip pen
Video player and cassette - pre-set.
Snack - if group is not bringing it.
Reading lamp or candle/matches, music cassette and player, for relaxation exercise (and for optional reflection). (Audiotape for session 2, if you prefer to use it instead of case studies.)

**CHECKLIST: Before session begins**
Set video at correct position and volume.
Make pencils available.
Set music cassette at correct position and volume.
Reading light plugged in and ready.
If you will be using a section of the Appendix, you may like to mark it with a bookmark or paper clip.

## 1. INTRODUCTION AND ICEBREAKER (3 mins)

**I'd like to make you all welcome to this session, which is about developing responsibility in children. This session builds on last week's, and I think you'll find it positive and practical.**

**We began to get to know each other last week, and it would be nice to get on first name terms with everyone as soon as possible, so maybe you'd like to change seats if you find you're sitting beside the same people as last week...?**

Allow time for people to re-seat themselves

**I wonder would each of you say what your name is, how many children you have, and what their age-range is...**

When all have introduced themselves, you might add, (with appropriate names):

**It's hard to remember all those names, so here's a game that can help - (Joe) here says, "I'm Joe." Next (Sharon) says "I'm Sharon and that's Joe." Then (Beth) says "I'm Beth and that's Sharon and that's Joe" And so on. Let's see how far we can get.**

Help anyone who gets stuck, bearing in mind that the laughter and "ice-breaking" is more important than remembering the names.

## SESSION TWO

If necessary, highlight any of the Agreements that may have been ignored during the previous meeting:

2. HOW WE GOT ON SINCE OUR LAST MEETING. (15-30 mins)
It may help to begin this section by recalling last week's plans. Don't be afraid of silence, because many people need time to gather their thoughts before speaking. A gentle look in the direction of one parent can often encourage that person to speak. Encourage any efforts or improvements - perhaps use active listening occasionally to reflect what someone says.

**Last week, we looked at some ways in which children hook us into their problems, and we saw that what *we* do often reinforces the misbehaviour instead of stopping it. At the end of the session we planned to try at least one new approach, maybe the opposite to what we normally do. So I wonder how you got on with that, or how have things been in your family over the past week...?**

Don't worry if people do not stay with the topic - the important thing is that they speak personally. The sharing during this section of the session is so important that much of the success of the course will depend on it. So it may help to go first on this occasion, sharing something that you yourself have done. If you do, remember to be brief - and not to be too "perfect." Mentioning a mistake you made, or something that didn't work out well, can often be as helpful as mentioning successes. (A very quiet group may prefer to talk first in pairs for a few minutes.)

3. GETTING IN TOUCH WITH THE NEW TOPIC (5-10 mins)
**In this session we'll be looking at how to help children become more responsible. To get us into the topic, we'll take a minute or two to look at the list of things in the "Getting in touch" section at the end of Chapter Two. You can tick off anything you usually do which your children might be capable of doing...**

After a minute or so, you can say:

**You can take a few minutes now to talk together in twos or threes about anything that strikes you in that list.**

After a few minutes, you can move on to the video.

4. INTRODUCING THE TOPIC (about 10 mins)

The videocassette for Session 2 may now be played. (When the video is not available, you may use the alternative introduction to the topic from Appendix 1 at the back of this Guide.)

After watching the video, participants can be encouraged to look at Table 2 and talk in pairs for a minute or so about their reaction to the ideas (the talking may be best in pairs and not in the full group for the first few sessions, so that people who feel shy don't feel under threat). If there is time, you may like to gather a few comments, but do not delay long on discussion, as the ideas and their implications usually become clearer with the case studies and skill practice. After a minute or so, move on to the Case Studies.

5. CASE STUDIES (about 10 mins)

**We'll look at the "Case Studies" now at the end of chapter 2, and we'll take a minute or two on each of the situations.**

This exercise can be done in groups of three - or the parents may enjoy taking parts and reading the situations aloud. If you are asked questions, help people to make their own decisions by turning back the question - even if their choices are different to what you would choose. Discussing the case studies will often widen the parents' horizons and help them see that there is not just one way to handle a situation. For this section you may like to use the audio-tapes (supplied with earlier editions of this programme), but an advantage of using the case studies from the handbook is that people are speaking in their *own* accents and tend to find it easier to enter into role-play situations later.

6. SKILL PRACTICE (15- 20 mins)

For session two, this section does not actually offer skill practice, but it is a significant group exercise. Put newsprint or a large sheet of blank paper on the wall (or floor) and ask group members:
**What responsibilities do you think a ten-year-old child is capable of around the house?** (or a younger or older child, depending on the average age of the children of those present). **You may find it helpful to look at the list of responsibilities in the "Getting in touch" section.**

# SESSION TWO

In groups with a wide age-range this exercise can be done twice, once for a five year old and, for example, once for a fifteen-year-old. All suggestions can be jotted down on the chart, and will invariably lead to some practical discussion.

**Well, that may help to lead us into our plans for the week ahead.**

2.35

## 7. PLANNING FOR THE WEEK AHEAD. (4-6 mins)

Suggest to everyone that they look at the chart and decide how they could begin to introduce one or two things from that list or from the list in the "Getting in touch" section.

**I'd like to give you a chance to think about how you might introduce one or two ideas from this chart into your own family - or even any of the things from the list in the "Getting in touch" section. Look at the Planning section and take a minute or two to plan quietly on your own. It may be a good idea to write down what you plan so that you remember it when you go home.**

After a minute or so you can continue:

**You can talk in pairs about your plan now and to tell each other what you intend to do - telling someone what you have planned usually helps to make it happen! Couples may prefer to plan together at this stage.**

If there is time, you might encourage a few parents to share their plans. After about two minutes you could move on to the reflection.

## 8. RELAXATION (AND OPTIONAL REFLECTION) 4-10 mins.

2.45

**We're coming to the end of the session now, so we'll have a quietening down time and a short reflection. I'll change the lighting and put on some background music to help you relax, and you're asked to sit comfortably, perhaps keep your back straight, and put both feet on the ground so that you're more grounded - close your eyes if that helps, and breathe more deeply and slowly...**

Pause for 20 seconds, before reading, with appropriate pauses:

**Would you like to try now to tense up your shoulders just a tiny little bit... Can you feel the tension...? Now relax them slowly... Feel the relaxation... Next, make your shoulders a *little* more tense, as if you were a bit nervous. Now, you're not terribly tense, but you'll**

notice the muscles across your back are *quite* tensed up. Many people carry their tensions and worries around like this all day long. It's quite draining. It's draining for *you*, but it's also unhelpful for your *child*, because children are remarkably sensitive to how you're feeling and can pick up the vibes when you're relaxed and when you're tense. So this tensing and relaxing exercise is something you might try regularly at home - maybe before you go to sleep at night, or when you find yourself tense during the day...

Read the following slowly, pausing briefly where there are continuous dots:

Now let's take a few moments to imagine ourselves putting into practice the plans we've just made to help our children take on some new responsibilities. Remember what you've planned... Can you zone in on one child, and see the face... What is she or he wearing...? Can you imagine the scene, and see yourself in it... What will help your child to be more willing and responsive... See yourself being supportive and encouraging, especially when it's difficult... (longer pause) And when you're ready, you can come back slowly to the room we're in and open your eyes and relax... (pause).

Let the music fade out gradually - do not switch it off abruptly. If you are using the optional religious dimension, however, let the music continue to play and read the reflection, using the text from appendix 2. Those not wanting to include a religious dimension may like to look at it and consider ways of adapting it.

## 9. SUMMING-UP. (5-10 mins)       *2.55*

To finish our meeting, I want to give you a chance to say whatever is on your mind, or what you plan to do, or how you're feeling now about the course. Whatever you need to say..

If you are pressed for time, you can ask people to say in one word how they are feeling. It may also help to say how *you* are feeling. What you say can be encouraging, but feel free to mention disappointment, for example, if little is happening between sessions. An "I" message like this can have quite a powerful effect on the group.

## 10. CONCLUDING REMARKS (1 min).

**For next week we're asked to read Chapter 3. You're also asked to look up our plans at home and work at them during the week. Finally, can we have a volunteer for the snack for next week?**

## AFTER THE MEETING.

Again the questions for evaluation with your co-leader: Did we talk too much? Did we answer questions or toss them back to the group? Are group members beginning to look to themselves for answers? What problems are we experiencing? What can we do about that? Who needs encouragement? What will we do differently next week?

It can also help to talk with other group leaders between sessions.

# SESSION THREE

**CHECKLIST: Materials**
Your leader's guide.
Your parents' handbook
Pencils or pens (preferably pencils).
Video player and cassette.
Snack - if group is not bringing it.
Reading lamp or candle/matches, music
cassette and player, for relaxation
exercise (and for optional reflection).
(Audiotape for session 3, if you prefer to
use it instead of case studies.)

**CHECKLIST: Before session begins**
Set video at correct position and volume.
Make pencils available.
Set music cassette at correct position
and volume.
Reading light plugged in and ready.
If you will be using a section of the
Appendix, you may like to mark it with a
bookmark or paper clip.
You might ask two members to prepare
for section 5 *before* meeting begins.

## 1. INTRODUCTION. (1 min)

Make members of the group welcome, especially anyone who missed
last week's meeting- in order to help make them feel part of the group.
Encourage people to sit beside people on both sides whom they have not
been sitting next to in the previous sessions. If necessary, ask the group
to look once again at the Agreements at the end of their book, and
highlight one that may have been ignored during the previous meeting.

## 2. HOW WE GOT ON. (15-30 mins)

It helps to begin this section with a brief recap of the previous session,
perhaps something like:

**So far we've looked at two things that may help parents. The first
was simply not to do what we usually do when our children
misbehave - not to give the attention, to ignore the squabbling or the
tantrums, to withdraw from an argument - but to deal with the
child's needs later. The second thing was gradually to give children
more responsibility, more choices. Last week, we planned at the end
of the session how we might start doing that in a small way with at
least one child, and I wonder how you got on? Or how have things
been going with your children in general?**

# SESSION THREE

Don't be afraid of silence, because many people need time to gather their thoughts together before speaking. A gentle look in the direction of one parent can often encourage that person to speak. And don't worry if people do not stay with the topic - the important thing is that they speak personally. Encourage any efforts or improvements.


## 3. GETTING IN TOUCH WITH THE NEW TOPIC (5-10 mins)

**Well, thank you for sharing that with the group. We'll move on now to this (evening's) topic, which is Encouragement. And we'll get into the topic by taking a minute or two to look at the "Getting in touch" section at the end of Chapter 3... And when you've ticked it off, you can take a few minutes to talk together in twos or threes about anything that strikes you there.**

There may be a question about the difference between praise and encouragement, but you are not there as a teacher so you might just refer parents to the section of chapter 3 entitled "The difference between praise and encouragement." or mention that it will probably become clearer when they see the video (or hear the alternative explanation from Appendix 1).

After a few minutes, you can move on to the video.


## 4. INTRODUCING THE TOPIC (about 10 mins)

The videocassette for Session 3 may now be played. (When the video is not available, you may use the alternative introduction to the topic from Appendix 1 at the back of this Guide.)

After watching the video, participants can be encouraged to look at Table 3 and talk in pairs for a minute or so about their reaction to the ideas (the talking may be best in pairs and not in the full group for the first few sessions, so that people who feel shy don't feel under threat). If there is time, you may like to gather a few comments, but do not delay long on discussion, as the ideas and their implications usually become clearer with the case studies and skill practice. After a minute or so, move on to the Case Studies.


## 5. CASE STUDIES (about 10 mins)

This exercise can be done in groups of three.

*p29 my book* (handwritten marginal note)

SESSION THREE

**We'll look at the "Case Studies" now at the end of chapter 3, and we'll take a minute or two on each of the situations.**

Alternatively, the parents may enjoy taking parts and reading the situations aloud. Or you may like to use the audiotapes (supplied with earlier editions of this programme).

## 6. SKILL PRACTICE (about 20 mins)

Ask two volunteers to act a short scene (the volunteers are best chosen from the more outgoing parents before the meeting starts). If they are reluctant, you may like to take one of the parts yourself. One will be a parent, the other a child, the parent is helping the child to put on a school tie/ to do maths homework/ to learn how to iron clothes (or some other skill, depending on the interest and age range of the children of those present). The parent is told to find fault, to criticise, to be impatient. The child is slow, resentful, fed-up. After a minute or so, ask how each felt. Ask the group how they felt as they watched.

*role play*

The same volunteers now act the same scene, but this time the parent is encouraging. After a minute or so, ask them, and then the other members of the group, how they felt this time.

**Well, any comments on that exercise or how did you feel about it?**

If the actors got into strong feelings, allow time to de-role - see the section on *Skill Practice* in the chapter "How this programme works."

## 7. PLANNING FOR THE WEEK AHEAD. (4-6 mins)

This is an opportunity for everyone to plan how they will apply the ideas from Session Three over the next week. They can work quietly on their own and then, in pairs, tell each other what they plan to do. This can be introduced something like this:

**That brings us to the planning for next week. You could look at the section "Plans for next week" just after the "Getting in touch" exercise at the end of the chapter, and take a minute or two to plan. You might ask yourself - Whom do I see as my most discouraged child? So what exactly am I going to do to encourage that child over the next week? When? Where? And so on.**

After a minute or so, you could continue:

## SESSION THREE

**Maybe you'd like to talk in pairs now and tell each other what you intend to do. Couples may prefer to plan together at this stage.**

If there is time, you might encourage a few parents to share their plans. After a further two minutes you could move on to the reflection.

**8. RELAXATION (AND OPTIONAL REFLECTION) 4-8 mins.**
**We're coming to the end of the session now, so we'll have a quietening down time, and use our imagination a little. I'll put on some background music to help you relax, and you're asked to sit comfortably, but keeping your back straight - close your eyes if that helps, and breathe deeply and slowly...** (Pause for about 20 seconds.)

**There are lots of different ways to relax. Becoming aware of your breathing is just one of them. Last week, for example, we tried tensing muscles and then relaxing them. Or some people find it relaxing just to become *aware* of sensations in their bodies, so here's an exercise you can do now and perhaps try at home later**

Read slowly, with brief pauses at continuous dots.

**Become aware of your back touching the back of the chair... Next, don't move, just feel how your clothes are touching your shoulders - you may feel your shoulders relaxing as you become aware of that... Next, your hands resting in your lap... Next, your bottom on the chair... Now your feet on the ground - don't move them, just become aware of them... Again your back... your shoulders... your right hand... your left hand... your bottom... your left foot... your right foot... Once again - shoulders, back, and so on. Move around your body, becoming aware of each part briefly and then on to the next part. Try this for a minute or so...**

After a minute or so, continue reading, with appropriate pauses:

**Now let's take a few moments to imagine ourselves putting into practice the plans we've just made to encourage our children. Remember what you've planned... Can you zone in on one child, and see the face... What is she or he wearing...? Can you imagine the scene, and see yourself in it... See yourself smiling or touching or hugging or doing something thoughtful... Hear yourself saying a kind word... And when you're ready, you can come back slowly to the room we're in and open your eyes and relax...** (pause).

# SESSION THREE

Let the music fade out gradually, but, if you are using the optional religious dimension, let the music continue, and read the reflection, using the text from appendix 2.

## 9. SUMMING-UP. (5-10 mins)

**This (evening) we've been looking at how we might criticise our children less and encourage them more. So I'd like to give you a few minutes to say briefly whatever is on your mind, or how you're feeling now about the course. Whatever you need to say..**

If you are pressed for time, you can ask people to say in one word how they are feeling.

## 10. CONCLUDING REMARKS (1 min).

**For next week we're asked to have Chapter Four read. It's about listening, and can lead to some important breakthroughs with your children. I would also encourage you to look up your plan at home and work at encouraging during the week. At the end of a course, there are usually some parents who have made big improvements, and their secret lies in what they do between sessions; other parents have regrets at the end of the eight weeks and they say: "I wish I had taken the course more seriously and worked at the skills." I mention this now because I don't want you to have those regrets. Finally, can we have a volunteer for the snack for next week?**

## AFTER THE MEETING.

Again the questions for evaluation with your co-leader: Did we talk too much? Did we answer questions or toss them back to the group? Are group members beginning to look to themselves for answers? What problems are we experiencing? What can we do about that? Who needs encouragement? What will we do differently next week?

It can also help to talk with other group leaders between sessions.

# SESSION FOUR

1. INTRODUCTION. (1 min.)
Make members of the group welcome, including anyone who missed last
week's meeting. Encourage them to sit beside people on both sides whom
they have not been sitting next to in recent sessions.

2. HOW WE GOT ON SINCE OUR LAST MEETING. (15-30 mins)
It may help to begin this section by recalling last week's plans.
 **In the first session we were encouraged to deal with misbehaviour
by not doing what we usually do. The second session was about giving
more responsibility to our children. Then the third session dealt with
encouragement, which goes hand in hand with giving responsibility,
doesn't it. I'm sure you're beginning to notice that all these skills are
connected, although it may be the end of the course before you can
see how they all tie together. So I wonder how you got on with your
plans to encourage one or more of your children this week? Or how
have things been going in general with your children...?**

3. GETTING IN TOUCH WITH THE NEW TOPIC (5-10 mins)
**Well, thank you for sharing that with the group. We'll move on now
to this (evening's) topic, which is Listening. And we'll get into the**

**topic by taking a minute or two to look at the "Getting in touch"
section at the end of Chapter 4...** P. 37

It may help to read the "Getting in Touch" section aloud. By session
four most people have lost their inhibitions about speaking in the larger
group, so, instead of asking people to work in pairs, you might ask the
group what they think the child is thinking and feeling in each case.
Otherwise, encourage them to talk in twos or threes.

You can then move on to the video.

## 4. INTRODUCING THE TOPIC (about 10 mins)

The videocassette for Session 4 may now be played. (When the video is
not available, you may use the alternative introduction to the topic from
Appendix 1 at the back of this Guide.)

After watching the video, participants can be encouraged to look at
Table 4 and talk in pairs for a minute or so about their reaction to the
ideas. Then move on to the Case Studies.

## 5. CASE STUDIES (about 10 mins)    P. 39

**We'll look at the "Case Studies" now at the end of chapter 4, and
we'll take a minute or two on each of the situations.**

This exercise can be done in groups of three - or the parents may
enjoy taking parts and reading the situations aloud. Or you may like to
use the audiotapes (supplied with earlier editions of this programme).

## 6. SKILL PRACTICE (10-20 mins)

Divide the group into pairs, preferably splitting couples and close friends
- unless they have reservations about that. If there is an odd number,
leave yourself out. Explain:

**I want you to decide who is the listener and who is the speaker in
each pair. It doesn't matter, because you'll have turns at both. The
speakers can speak about a real or imaginary worry or concern they
have - about their children or about anything at all. A real worry is
better because it's easier to talk about, but you decide. Or you could
talk about a conflict you had, or a misunderstanding, with a
neighbour or a brother or sister or mother-in- law... Tell how the
conflict started and how you felt at each stage and what you've done**

about it and so on. The listener's task is to try to give the speaker an experience of being understood - by using helpful silences, a suitable tone of voice, helpful comments, active listening and so on. So please don't solve the problem, or offer advice, or interrupt. After a few minutes, I'll stop the exercise and the speakers can tell you what helped them to feel understood and what didn't help. Then the listeners become the speakers and we'll do the same all over again with a different problem or worry, perhaps about their children. Okay? So the speakers can start explaining their worry now...

After 3 minutes, allow the speakers to talk about what helped and hindered their sense of being understood. Then, after another minute or so, reverse the roles and do the exercise again.

I wonder how you found that whole exercise - what helped you to talk and to feel understood, or what did you learn from it...?

## 7. PLANNING FOR NEXT WEEK. (4-6 mins)

This is an opportunity for everyone to plan how they will apply the ideas from Session Four over the next week. They can work quietly on their own and then, in pairs, tell each other what they plan to do. This can be introduced something like this:

That brings us straight into the planning for next week. You've just had a few minutes of undivided attention from another person listening to you and the suggestion is that we might also give a few minutes of completely undivided attention to one of our children during next week. That's easier said than done - it will usually need to be planned. So we'll look at the "Plans for next week." section of the book and take a minute or so to read that. And we'll plan quietly on our own what we can do to give one of our children a good experience of being listened to during the week. Timing is obviously important - like bedtime, or when they're worried about something. And being specific helps - not asking, "How's school?" (which may be too general) so much as "Who's on the team?" It may be a good idea to write down what you plan to do. That way, you can look it up at home and remind yourself of what you've planned. And in planning, remember that the more specific you are the better. You can ask yourself - **What exactly am I going to do this week? When? Who with? And so on.**

After a minute or so, you could continue:

**Maybe you'd like to talk in pairs about your plan now and to tell each other what you intend to do. As usual, couples may prefer to plan together at this stage.**

After a further two minutes you could move on to the reflection.

## 8. RELAXATION (AND OPTIONAL REFLECTION) 4-10 mins.

**We're coming to the end of the session now, so we'll have our quiet time. I'll put on some background music to help you relax, and you're asked to sit comfortably, perhaps keeping your back straight - close your eyes if that helps, and breathe deeply and slowly...**

Pause for 20 seconds, before reading, with appropriate pauses:

**We saw in an earlier session that deep breathing - or even becoming *aware* of our breathing - can help us to slow down and relax. Let's try a variation on that - take a slow, deep breath as you count to four... hold it for one two, three, four... and slowly, gently, let it out, counting to eight... In... two three, four, hold it, two, three, four... and gently empty your lungs, two, three, four, five, six, seven, eight... Keep doing that for a minute or so, and feel yourself relaxing...**

**Well, we all need to find ways of coping with the stresses and strains of parenting, so what we've just done is one more way to try out at home and see what helps *you* to relax.**

Read the following slowly, pausing at the continuous dots:

**Now let's take a few moments to imagine ourselves putting into practice the plans we've just made to give our children a better experience of being listened to this week. Remember what you've planned... Now, set the scene, the time, the place... And see yourself and your child in it... What will help you to listen better...? See yourself listening and notice the difference it's beginning to make to your relationship with the child... (longer pause) And when you're ready, you can come back slowly to the room we're in and relax...**

Let the music fade out gradually, but, if you are using the optional religious dimension, let the music continue, and read the reflection, using the text from appendix 2.

## 9. SUMMING-UP. (5-10 mins)

**This (evening) we've been looking at ways of improving our listening, especially our "active listening". So to finish our meeting, maybe you'd like to take a few minutes to say where you are with all that or how you're feeling now at the end of this session. Whatever you need to say...**

If you are pressed for time, you can ask people to say in one word how they are feeling.

## 10. CONCLUDING REMARKS (1 min).

**For next week we're asked to have Chapter Five read. Maybe some of you feel that, when there's a problem in the family, listening isn't always the answer. And you're right - listening helps with some problems, and it's a good starting point. But the next chapter looks at where we can go from there, and how we can deal with a problem once we *have* done some listening. You may find it helpful to read that chapter a number of times before the next session, because, although it's only a few pages, there's a lot in it. And I would also encourage you all, as usual, to look up your plans at home and work on them during the week. Finally, can we have a volunteer for the snack for next week?**

## AFTER THE MEETING.

Again the questions for evaluation with your co-leader: Did we talk too much? Did we answer questions or toss them back to the group? Are group members beginning to look to themselves for answers? What problems are we experiencing? What can we do about that? Who needs encouragement? What will we do differently next week?

# SESSION FIVE

**CHECKLIST: Materials**
Your leader's guide.
Your parents' handbook
Pencils or pens (preferably pencils).
Video player and cassette.
Snack - if group is not bringing it.
Reading lamp or candle/matches, music
cassette and player, for relaxation
exercise (and for optional reflection).
(Audiotape for session 5, if you prefer to
use it instead of case studies.)

**CHECKLIST: Before session begins**
Set video at correct position and volume.
Make pencils available.
Set music cassette at correct position
and volume.
Reading light plugged in and ready.
If you will be using a section of the
Appendix, you may like to mark it with a
bookmark or paper clip.

## 1. INTRODUCTION. (1 min.)
Make members of the group welcome, including anyone who missed last
week's meeting. Encourage them to sit beside people on both sides whom
they have not been sitting next to in recent sessions.

## 2. HOW WE GOT ON. (15-30 mins)
It helps to begin this section by recalling last week's plans.

**Last week we saw that when someone has a problem, when a child
is upset about his broken toy or crying because her big sister pulled
her hair, or depressed about having no friends, what that child
probably needs most is *listening*, a sense of being understood. So let's
see how we got on this week with our plans to improve our listening -
or how have things been going in general with your children?**
Make sure to encourage any efforts or improvements.

## 3. GETTING IN TOUCH WITH THE NEW TOPIC (5-10 mins) P.45
**Well, thank you for sharing that with the group. We'll move on now
to this (evening's) topic, which is about managing problems. And
we'll get into the topic by trying to decide who owns each of the
problems in the "Getting in touch" section at the end of Chapter 5...**

# SESSION FIVE

You may prefer to work with the larger group rather than in pairs. For each of the situations you could ask:

**Who owns the problem?**

It's important to be flexible in doing this exercise, recognising that *both* parent and child sometimes own the problem. In a case like that, you could ask: Who *most* owns the problem?

You can then move on to the video.

## 4. INTRODUCING THE TOPIC (about 10 mins)

The videocassette for Session 5 may now be played. (When the video is not available, you may use the alternative introduction to the topic from Appendix 1 at the back of this Guide.)

After watching the video, participants can be encouraged to look at Table 5 and talk in pairs for a minute or so about their reaction to the ideas. Then move on to the Case Studies. P. 46 - 47

## 5. CASE STUDIES (about 10 mins)

**We'll look at the "Case Studies" now at the end of chapter 5, and we'll take a minute or two on each of the situations.**

This exercise can be done in groups of three - or the parents may enjoy taking parts and reading the situations aloud. Or you may like to use the audiotapes (supplied with earlier editions of this programme).

## 6. SKILL PRACTICE (10-20 mins)

Divide the group into pairs, preferably splitting couples and close friends unless they have reservations about that. If there is an odd number you can leave yourself out. Introduce the exercise something like this:

**I'd like one of you to take one or two minutes to describe to your partner a problem situation in your own family where your child owns the problem. If you're stuck for ideas, you could look at the list in the "Getting in Touch" section of your books...** (2 mins)

After two minutes you could say:

**Now I want you to act as your own child, and I want your partner to take you through the four stages for managing problems as in chapter five. We'll take four minutes for that - though it might take much longer at home!...** (4 mins)

If there is time, allow the *other* person in each pairing to describe a problem situation and to deal with it in the same way.

When this exercise has been done, you might ask:

**Well, how did that go, or how did you feel about it?**

## 7. PLANNING FOR THE WEEK AHEAD. (4-6 mins)

**That brings us to the planning for next week. You could look at the section "Plans for next week" at the end of the chapter, and take a minute or two to plan.** (1-2 mins)      P.45

**Maybe you'd like to talk in pairs now and tell each other what you intend to do. (Couples may prefer to plan together at this stage.)**

If there is time, you might encourage a few parents to share their plans. After a further two minutes you could move on to the reflection.

## 8. RELAXATION (AND OPTIONAL REFLECTION) 4-10 mins.

**We're coming to the end of the session now, so we'll have our quiet time. I'll put on some background music to help you relax, and you're asked to sit comfortably, perhaps keeping your back straight - close your eyes if that helps, and breathe deeply and slowly...**

Pause for 20 seconds, before reading, with appropriate pauses:

**Last week, we tried breathing more deeply, which is one way of relaxing, but it's not essential to breathe more deeply at all - even to become *aware* of my breathing is often a good way to relax. Try that now. Don't change the way you're breathing at all. Just concentrate on the inside of your nose and notice the cool air as it passes in through your nose, and the warm air as it passes out again...** (pause for about 20 seconds) **Concentrate on the air as it passes through your nose, in and out...** (another similar pause) **Empty your mind of everything else - if any thoughts or distractions come to you, don't struggle against them, recognise "I'm worrying about my child now," or whatever, but just put the thought aside and go on concentrating on your breathing for another minute or so...**

Read the following slowly, pausing briefly at continuous dots:

**Now let's take a few moments to imagine ourselves putting into practice the plans we've just made to do some respectful, constructive problem management with our children this week. Remember what**

51

**you've planned... Now, set the scene, the time, the place... And see
yourself and your child in it... What will help you to stay calm and
respectful...? See yourself helping the child to deal with the problem,
and notice the difference it makes...** (longer pause) **And when you're
ready, you can come back slowly to the room we're in and relax...**

Let the music fade out gradually, but, if you are using the optional
religious dimension, let the music continue, and read the reflection, using
the text from appendix 2.

## 9. SUMMING-UP. (5-10 mins)

**In this session we've been looking at how and when to use "I"
messages, when to use active listening, and how to communicate with
our children about problems, using the four stages. So maybe you'd
like to say where you are with all that now, or how you're feeling now
at the end of this session. Whatever you need to say..**

If you are pressed for time, you can ask people to say in one word
how they are feeling.

## 10. CONCLUDING REMARKS (1 min).

**For next week we're asked to have Chapter Six read. It deals with
discipline, and what action we can take when talking doesn't seem to
work. And I look forward to hearing next week how you get on with
your plans. Can we have a volunteer for the snack for next week...?**

## AFTER THE MEETING.

Again the questions for evaluation with your co-leader: Did we talk too
much? Did we answer questions or toss them back to the group? Are
group members beginning to look to themselves for answers? What
problems are we experiencing? What can we do about that? Who needs
encouragement? What will we do differently next week?

# SESSION SIX

**CHECKLIST: Materials**
Your leader's guide.
Your parents' handbook
Pencils or pens (preferably pencils).
Video player and cassette.
Snack - if group is not bringing it.
Reading lamp or candle/matches, music
cassette and player, for relaxation
exercise (and for optional reflection).
(Audiotape for session 6, if you prefer to
use it instead of case studies.)

**CHECKLIST: Before session begins**
Set video at correct position and volume.
Make pencils available.
Set music cassette at correct position
and volume.
Reading light plugged in and ready.
If you will be using a section of the
Appendix, you may like to mark it with a
bookmark or paper clip.
You may like to choose 1-2 volunteers
for the skill practice (see section 5).

## 1. INTRODUCTION. (1 min.)

Make members of the group welcome, including anyone who missed last week's meeting. Encourage them to sit beside people on both sides whom they have not been sitting next to in recent sessions.

## 2. HOW WE GOT ON SINCE OUR LAST MEETING. (15-30 mins)

It helps to begin this section by recalling last week's plans. It may help, too, to share your own experience of using "I" messages or the stages of managing problems – but don't be too perfect!

**Last week we made some plans to use "I" messages - or to try using the four stages with a child or a partner. So I wonder how you all got on with that, or how things have been going in general with your children?**

Make sure to encourage any efforts or improvements.

## 3. GETTING IN TOUCH WITH THE NEW TOPIC (5-10 mins)   P 54.

**Well, thank you for sharing that with the group. We'll move on now to this (evening's) topic, which is Discipline. And we'll get into the topic by looking at the "Getting in Touch" section of chapter six. What do parents normally do when a child throws a tantrum...?**

# SESSION SIX

Help members of the group to decide what parents normally do in each case. You can then move on to the video.

## 4. INTRODUCING THE TOPIC (about 10 mins)
The videocassette for Session 6 may now be played. (When the video is not available, you may use the alternative introduction to the topic from Appendix 1 at the back of this Guide.)

After watching the video, participants can be encouraged to look at Table 6 and talk in pairs for a minute or so about their reaction to the ideas. Then move on to the Case Studies.

## 5. CASE STUDIES (about 10 mins) *p.56*
**We'll look at the "Case Studies" now at the end of chapter 6, and we'll take a minute or two on each of the situations.**

This exercise can be done in groups of three - or the parents may enjoy taking parts and reading the situations aloud. Or you may like to use the audiotapes (supplied with earlier editions of this programme).

## 6. SKILL PRACTICE (20-25 mins)
Before the meeting choose two volunteers, A and B. A now describes a real parent-child problem situation from A's own family - what the child does and says and what (s)he (the parent) does and says. Next, A acts the part of her/his own child while B acts the part of the parent. (If you have had difficulty in getting volunteers, you might try this role yourself).

Stop the role-play once the situation is quite clear and ask A to leave the room for one or two minutes, explaining that the group is going to try to come up with some suggestions. Together, the rest of the group now brainstorm on the best way to apply consequences to the situation. Help them to choose a solution.

When A returns to the room, B acts once again as the parent and this time applies the consequences that the group has chosen.

Ask A and B how they felt in the new role-play and ask for brief comments from the group.

If people are reluctant to try this exercise, it can be discussed, brainstormed, and a solution chosen - though the learning tends to be greater when it is acted.

## 7. PLANNING FOR THE WEEK AHEAD. (4-6 mins)

**That brings us to the planning for next week. You could look at the planning section at the end of the chapter, and take a minute or two to plan.** (1-2 mins)

**Maybe you'd like to talk in pairs now and tell each other what you intend to do. (Couples may prefer to plan together at this stage.)**

If there is time, you might encourage a few parents to share their plans. After a further two minutes you could move on to the reflection.

## 8. RELAXATION (AND OPTIONAL REFLECTION) 4-10 mins.

**We're coming to the end of the session now, so we'll have our quiet time. I'll put on some background music to help you relax, and you're asked to sit comfortably, perhaps keeping your back straight - close your eyes if that helps, and breathe deeply and slowly...**

Pause for 20 seconds, before reading, with appropriate pauses:

**Would you like now to tense up your shoulders until they're *quite* tense, and hold them there...** (brief pause.) **And slowly release the tension and relax - feel the tension easing out of your body...** (pause.) **Try it again? - shoulders tensed...** (brief pause.) **And slowly release the tension again - feel your body relaxing...** (pause.) **Next, try tensing up the muscles in your thighs... hold it there...** (brief pause.) **Now slowly relax...** (pause) **Try it again? - tense... hold it...** (brief pause.) **And slowly relax...** (pause.)

**I'd remind you that you can do this kind of tensing and relaxing exercise with different parts of the body at home - if you're finding it difficult to go to sleep at night, or whenever you find yourself tense during the day.**

Read the following slowly, pausing briefly at continuous dots:

**Next, let's take a few moments to imagine ourselves putting into practice the plans we've just made to help our children learn to discipline themselves. Now, see yourself offering a choice to your child... Notice how calm and respectful you are - there's no aggression or punishment in your voice... Be happy with your child's choice... Be content to see your child making a decision, and living with consequences, and learning self-discipline... And when you're ready, you can come back slowly to the room we're in and relax...**

Let the music fade out gradually, but, if you are using the optional religious dimension, let the music continue, and read the reflection, using the text from appendix 2.

## 9. SUMMING-UP. (5-10 mins)

**In this session we've been looking at ways of dealing with problem situations, not by punishing children or rewarding them, but by offering them choices and generally letting them live with the consequences of their decisions. So maybe you'd like to say where you are with all that now, or how you're feeling at the end of this session - or anything else you'd like to mention...**

If you are pressed for time, you can ask people to say in one word how they are feeling.

## 10. CONCLUDING REMARKS (1 min).

**For next week we're asked to have Chapter Seven read. It deals with Family Meetings, which many people think are the best guarantee that what we learn on this course will last. And can we have a volunteer for the snack for next week...?**

## AFTER THE MEETING.

Again the questions for evaluation with your co-leader: Did we talk too much? Did we answer questions or toss them back to the group? Are group members beginning to look to themselves for answers? What problems are we experiencing? What can we do about that? Who needs encouragement? What will we do differently next week?

# SESSION SEVEN

**CHECKLIST: Materials**
Your leader's guide.
Your parents' handbook
Pencils or pens (preferably pencils).
Video player and cassette.
Snack - if group is not bringing it.
Reading lamp or candle/matches, music
cassette and player, for relaxation
exercise (and for optional reflection).
(Audiotape for session 7, if you prefer to
use it instead of case studies.)

**CHECKLIST: Before session begins**
Set video at correct position and volume.
Make pencils available.
Set music cassette at correct position
and volume.
Reading light plugged in and ready.
If you will be using a section of the
Appendix, you may like to mark it with a
bookmark or paper clip.
You may like to choose 1-2 volunteers
for the skill practice (see section 5).

1. INTRODUCTION. (1 min.)
Begin by making members of the group welcome, including anyone who
missed last week's meeting. Encourage them to sit beside people on both
sides whom they have not been sitting next to in recent sessions.

2. HOW WE GOT ON SINCE OUR LAST MEETING. (15-30 mins)
It helps to begin this section by recalling last week's plans.
**Last week, we looked at discipline, particularly offering children
choices and allowing them to live with the consequences of what they
choose. So I wonder how you got on this week, or how you've been
getting along with your children in general...?**

3. GETTING IN TOUCH WITH THE NEW TOPIC (5-10 mins)
**Well, thank you for sharing that with the group. We'll move on now
to this (evening's) topic, which is about talking things out in a family.
Let's start by looking at the "Getting in Touch" section of chapter 7.
Will you form groups of three to talk about it...**
If necessary, help to form groups. Allow a few minutes for
discussion. Then move on to the video.

## 4. INTRODUCING THE TOPIC (about 10 mins)

The videocassette for Session 7 may now be played. (When the video is not available, you may use the alternative introduction to the topic from Appendix 1 at the back of this Guide.) After watching the video, participants can look at Table 7 and talk in pairs for a minute or so about their reaction to the ideas. Then they can move on to the Case Studies.

## 5. CASE STUDIES (about 10 mins)

**We'll look at the "Case Studies" now at the end of chapter 7, and we'll take a minute or two on each of the situations.**

This exercise can be done in groups of three - or the parents may enjoy taking parts and reading the situations aloud. Or you may like to use the audiotapes (supplied with earlier editions of this programme).

## 6. SKILL PRACTICE (about 20 mins)

Ask three volunteers to hold a family meeting - one will be a parent and the other two will be children, with ages corresponding to the ages of children of group members. Or ask two volunteers to be the children and you could be the parent, if you don't mind trying that. Explain that you will run the meeting twice, the first time without using the skills taught on the programme and the second time using the skills. Decide together what you would like to discuss - planning a family outing, for example.

Discuss this subject in the normal way first. That will usually lead to a ragged discussion with a lot of disagreement, criticism and wrangling. After two minutes, stop it and ask how each one felt.

Then have a "family meeting" on the same topic. This time the "parent" can follow the stages in Table 7, using active listening, asking for suggestions and jot them down without reacting; then asking about the advantages and disadvantages of each suggestion and working towards a consensus. You can stop the meeting after a few minutes, allow those doing the role-play to say how they felt, and ask for comments/feelings from other members of the group.

## 7. PLANNING FOR THE WEEK AHEAD. (4-6 mins)

**You could look now at the planning section at the end of the chapter, and take a minute or two to plan.** (1-2 mins)

**Maybe you'd like to talk in pairs now and tell each other what you intend to do. (Couples may prefer to plan together at this stage.)**

If there is time, you might encourage a few parents to share their plans. After a further two minutes you could move on to the reflection.

## 8. RELAXATION (AND OPTIONAL REFLECTION) 4-10 mins.

**We're coming to the end of the session now, so we'll have our quiet time. I'll put on some background music to help you relax, and you're asked to sit comfortably, perhaps keeping your back straight - close your eyes if that helps, and breathe deeply and slowly... Notice the breath as you breathe in and notice it as you breathe out...** (30 secs)

Pause for 20 seconds, before reading, with appropriate pauses:

**Now a variation on some of the breathing exercises we've tried. As you breathe in and out, say to yourself a word that calms you, or makes you feel at peace. It might be the word "relax," or "peaceful," or "calm down." You can say the word as you breathe in *or* as you breathe out, or you can split it between the two, saying "calm," for example, as you breathe in, and "down" as you breathe out...** (30 secs)

**If you notice tension in any part of your body, concentrate on that part as you breathe in and out, saying your word...**

Pause for 30 seconds. Then, as you read, pause long enough at the continuous dots to allow people to imagine without being rushed.

**Now let's take a few moments to imagine ourselves putting into practice the plans we've just made to have some kind of family discussion to involve our children in the decisions that affect themselves. Remember what you've planned... Now, set the scene, the time, the place... And see yourself and your child in it... See yourself listening well... And also being assertive in saying what *you* need... What will help you to stay calm and respectful...? See yourself coming to an agreement that respects you both... and feel the different atmosphere in your home already... And when you're ready, you can come back slowly to the room we're in and relax...**

Let the music fade out gradually, but, if you are using the optional religious dimension, let the music continue, and read the reflection, using the text from appendix 2.

## 9. SUMMING-UP. (5-10 mins)

**In this session we've been looking at ways of having family discussions and involving our children in the decisions that affect them. Maybe you'd like to say where you are with all that now, or how you're feeling at the end of this session - or if there's anything else you'd like to mention...**

If you are pressed for time, you can ask people to say in one word how they are feeling.

## 10. CONCLUDING REMARKS (1 min).

**For next week we're asked to have Chapter Eight read. It brings all the skills of the course together, and we see how they can also be applied to other adults in our lives. I also look forward to hearing how you all get on with family meetings. And can we have a volunteer for the snack for next week...?**

## AFTER THE MEETING.

Again the questions for evaluation with your co-leader: Did we talk too much? Did we answer questions or toss them back to the group? Are group members beginning to look to themselves for answers? What problems are we experiencing? What can we do about that? Who needs encouragement? What will we do differently next week?

# SESSION EIGHT

**CHECKLIST: Materials**
Your leader's guide.
Your parents' handbook
Pencils or pens (preferably pencils).
Video player and cassette.
Snack - if group is not bringing it.
Reading lamp or candle/matches, music
cassette and player, for relaxation
exercise (and for optional reflection).
(Audiotape for session 8, if you prefer to
use it instead of case studies.)

**CHECKLIST: Before session begins**
Set video at correct position and volume.
Make pencils available.
Set music cassette at correct position
and volume.
Reading light plugged in and ready.
If you will be using a section of the
Appendix, you may like to mark it with a
bookmark or paper clip.
Sheets of paper and pencils (see sect. 5).

## 1. INTRODUCTION. (1 min.)

Make members of the group welcome, including anyone who missed last week's meeting. Encourage them to sit beside people on both sides whom they have not been sitting next to in recent sessions.

## 2. HOW WE GOT ON SINCE OUR LAST MEETING. (15-30 mins)

It helps to begin this section by recalling last week's plans.

**Last week, we planned to try some form of family meeting. I wonder how that went or how things have been going in general?**

## 3. GETTING IN TOUCH WITH THE NEW TOPIC (5-10 mins)

**Well, thank you for sharing that with the group. We'll move on now to this (evening's) topic. We're not learning any new skill in this session - just judging when to use one skill and when to use another. We'll start by looking at Table 8 in your books.** Pg. 71

Use the questions from the "Getting in Touch" section of chapter eight. Question 1 can be explored with the group. Then you can allow members to tackle questions 2 and 3 for a few minutes in pairs or threes.

**Anyone like to add a problem behaviour for the bottom space of column 1?"**

With the group, explore different possible approaches to one or two problem behaviours. Then move on to the video.

## 4. INTRODUCING THE TOPIC (about 10 mins)

The videocassette for Session 8 may now be played. (When the video is not available, you may use the alternative introduction to the topic from Appendix 1 at the back of this Guide.)

After watching the video, participants can be encouraged to look at Table 8 and talk in pairs for a minute or so about their reaction to the ideas. Then they can move on to the Case Studies.

## 5. CASE STUDIES (about 10 mins)

**We'll look at the "Case Studies" now at the end of chapter 8, and we'll take a minute or two on each of the situations.**

This exercise can be done in groups of three - or the parents may enjoy taking parts and reading the situations aloud. Or you may like to use the audiotapes (supplied with earlier editions of this programme).

## 6. SKILL PRACTICE (about 20 mins)

The following exercise tends to be a *most* encouraging one, and it is particularly appropriate for a final session. Give out a small sheet of paper to each member of the group and explain:

**So often we're aware of our weaknesses as people and as parents and we're not nearly aware enough of our strengths, so I'm going to ask you now to take two minutes to write down at least four or five strengths you have as a parent - any good qualities or skills you have... (1-2 mins)**

**Now take a few minutes to write down the name of each person in the group and beside that name one or two good things you see in that person as a parent - caring, gentleness, firmness, sense of humour, patience, or whatever... (about 3 mins)**

**Now I'd like to go around the group, starting with (Sonya). If you wouldn't mind reading out the strengths that you wrote down for yourself, Sonya, and then we'll ask anyone who likes to add to that.**

Allow more than half the members to speak each time as you move around each person in the group, but try to give everyone a chance to speak at least once. That will tend to allow each person to be affirmed by those who feel most positive about them, and it will also prevent the exercise from dragging on too long. When enough people have spoken each time, you could say something like:

**Sorry to cut in, but we'll have to move on now to (John).**

Leaders are encouraged also to participate, allowing others to point out their strengths. At the end of the exercise ask:

**Didn't you recognise that what was said about each person was *true* for that person? So it was true for you too. You do have those strengths, and the more you believe that, the more you have to give to your children.**

You might ask, depending on how much time you have:

**Any comments on that exercise or how did you feel about it...?**

## 7. PLANNING FOR THE WEEK AHEAD. (4-6 mins)

**You can look now at the "planning ahead" section and take a minute or two to plan how you might continue to improve your parenting skills over the next few months... (1-2 mins)**

**Maybe you'd like to talk in pairs now and tell each other what you intend to do. (Couples may prefer to plan together at this stage.)**

If there is time, you might encourage a few parents to share their plans. After a further two minutes you can move on to the reflection.

## 8. RELAXATION (AND OPTIONAL REFLECTION) 4-10 mins.

**We're coming to the end of the session now, so we'll have our quiet time. I'll put on some background music to help you relax, and you're asked to sit comfortably, perhaps keeping your back straight - close your eyes if that helps, and breathe deeply and slowly... Notice the breath as you breathe in and notice it as you breathe out...**

Pause for 20 seconds, before reading, with appropriate pauses:

**For the relaxation exercise this (evening) you may try any of the relaxation exercises you have found helpful - a breathing exercise, or a tensing and relaxing exercise, or becoming aware of a part of your body, or imagining yourself in some pleasant place where you look around and listen to sounds and feel the sun or the breeze, or saying a word that calms you and makes you feel at peace. Whatever helps. Just choose one and relax with it... (1-2 mins)**

Read the following slowly, pausing briefly at continuous dots:

**Now let's take a few moments to imagine ourselves putting into practice the plans we've just made. What is the single change you most want to introduce into your family over the next few weeks and months...? Can you see yourself in that changed scene...? Focus on yourself, because change in the family begins with a change in you - see yourself more calm and respectful... Feel the difference in the atmosphere in your home... And when you're ready, you can come back slowly to the room we're in and relax...**

Let the music fade out gradually, but, if you are using the optional religious dimension, let the music continue, and read the reflection, using the text from appendix 2.

## 9. SUMMING-UP. (5-10 mins)

**In this session we've been trying to see how the various parenting skills fit together, and also how we might use them in dealing with *adults* as well as children. Maybe you'd like to say where you are with all that now, or how you're feeling at the end of this session - or if there's anything else you'd like to mention...**

If you are pressed for time, you can ask people to say in one word how they are feeling.

## 10. PRESENTATION OF CERTIFICATES. 7 questions

Conclude with a word of appreciation for the efforts parents have made and the improvements you have seen in them.

The certificates of completion of the course can be presented at the end of the session - or just after the Reflection and before the summing up. Alternatively, they can be presented at a special ceremony for a number of parent groups. This can mean a lot to them, especially if they have had little recognition for educational achievement in their lives.

It may be useful also to do a short evaluation at the end of the course, perhaps to ask everyone to write down the thing that they liked most or which they gained most from the course, and the thing that most disappointed them or that they most disliked. This is best done without discussion beforehand so that they are not unduly influenced by others. If the same "dislike" occurs consistently, that may indicate something that needs to be changed in the presentation of the course.

## SESSION EIGHT

### FOLLOW-UP

Many people request follow-up after completing this parenting course, and the ideal follow-up is probably something that reinforces the same skills as the parenting programme itself.

Some groups continue to meet to go through the entire course again - and many of them claim that they get much more out of it the second time around! The original leader(s) do not have to belong to this ongoing support group: a different person can even take responsibility for running each session, so that the leadership is revolved and more people involved. In some areas, people who complete this second course are invited to join the local parenting "team" - and being part of the team can mean anything from assisting in running courses to helping with a baby-sitting service for parents who wish to attend the programme.

For parents of teenagers, an obvious follow-up is the six-session 'Parenting Teenagers' Programme. Indeed, it is recommended that parents of teenagers do the Fives to Fifteens programme first - so that the 'Parenting Teenagers' Programme will be an opportunity for them to reinforce the same skills.

Most people do not want continuous ongoing support but may learn a great deal from further short courses. You may like to write to Family Caring Trust for a brochure with details of additional courses on family relationships.

# APPENDIX 1: WHEN YOU CANNOT USE THE VIDEO.

*There may be occasions when it will be impossible for you to use a video. Below is an alternative, replacing section four, "Introducing the Topic," and generally based on the tables in the parents' handbook.*

SESSION ONE

**Normally you'll have had a chance to read the chapter in advance, but obviously for this first meeting you haven't had that chance. So, working now from this Leader's Guide, I'll make a brief summary of what's in chapter one.**

**The chapter looks at children's misbehaviour, and we see that children usually don't know why they're misbehaving, but that it's usually because they're discouraged, and because of a mistaken belief that this is the only way they can get attention, or power, or whatever. But the chapter encourages us to look at *ourselves*, not just at the child, and we see that we often *reward* misbehaviour and reinforce it by *noticing* it, by giving attention on demand, by scolding, shouting, threatening, or whatever. I think that comes out fairly clearly in Table One, if you'd like to look at it now. In the first column the child is laying the bait - not deliberately, because we've just seen that children are just discouraged and aren't normally *aware* of what they're doing. The second column shows what the child is probably seeking - we're all aware, I'm sure, of how much attention-seeking goes on (though it's not just attention-seeking, it's attention-*needing* too, isn't it)? When a child doesn't get this attention, that often develops into the second stage there, a power contest. And when parents constantly win power contests, that can easily develop into the third stage, which is revenge-seeking. Or a very discouraged child will often show inadequacy, which is the fourth example there. And finally the fifth example, approval of friends, which becomes more important to children as they get older.**

**If you look at the third column, you can see there what parents often do in these situations, and it's pretty obvious, I think, that what they're doing is just not effective, because the misbehaviour is being rewarded instead of being stopped.**

The fourth column offers some suggestions as to what parents might do instead, to become more effective. To sum up, the suggestion is that you try taking a new approach or even doing the *opposite* to what you normally do.

There's no guarantee that doing the opposite to what you normally do is going to work for you. But if the approach you're using at the moment isn't working, this course encourages you to try other approaches until you find one that *does* work for you. If what we're doing now isn't working, then we've nothing to lose with a new approach, and it's usually fascinating in session two to hear how parents *did* get on when they tried a new approach.

You could invite the parents to look at Table One for a further minute or two. Then continue:

Now you don't have to remember what's in this Table, but I wonder if you can see how these ideas might apply to yourself, or how you could apply them in your own family...?

If people react to Table One, or are critical of these ideas, please respect their right to disagree, and do not try to teach, argue or defend.


SESSION TWO
I'll make a brief summary of what's in chapter 2, working from the Leader's Guide.

A psychologist called Rudolf Dreikurs noticed that children become more responsible when they are *given* responsibility, so one of his guidelines for parents is: *Do not do for children what children are capable of doing for themselves.* By making so many decisions for our children and doing so much for them, making beds, ironing shirts, buttoning buttons, making school lunches, tying laces, and so on, we may be encouraging our children to become irresponsible instead of responsible. So the suggestion in Chapter 2 is that we take time to *train* our children gradually to take on responsibilities, so that they will grow up to become responsible, caring, co-operative adults. That means letting go of some of the things we tend to control now, and allowing the children to do them. It also means giving them greater

**freedom to choose and to make decisions for themselves. If you'd like to look at Table 2, you'll see some examples of what we mean...**

Read down through the Table if you suspect the parents have poor reading skills; otherwise, give them a minute or two to read it and then ask any of the following questions:

**Any comments on this idea of giving children more responsibility?**

**Can you see how any of these ideas apply to you, or how you could apply them in *your* family...?**


SESSION THREE

**I'll make a brief summary of what's in chapter 3, working from the Leader's Guide. We see in the chapter that many parents, in an effort to improve their children, regularly criticise and find fault. We have to correct children, of course, but continually pointing out their mistakes tends to discourage them - and usually has the *opposite* effect. Psychologists tell us that behaviour that's noticed tends to *increase*, whereas behaviour that's ignored tends to *decrease*. The suggestion, then, is that we might sometimes postpone correction until a suitable time and that we begin looking out, not for mistakes, but for efforts, improvements and co-operation.**

**There is a section in the chapter on the difference between praise and encouragement. Praise tends to exaggerate - "You're absolutely wonderful!" or to give *my* opinion instead of helping children to *discover* their own strengths and improvements. A child will often feel more comfortable and encouraged by a low-key remark that just *notices* her contribution - "Oh good, you hung up your coat."**

**Table 3 is a kind of summary of these ideas. If you'd like to look at it, you'll see some examples of what we mean... Maybe we'll just take a minute or two to read down through it, and if you'd like to make any comments, feel free to do so.**

Allow time for reading the page and then ask:

**I wonder if anybody would like to make any comment about that Table or can you see how it might apply in your own family...?**

Move on fairly quickly to the Case Studies.

# APPENDIX 1: WHEN YOU CANNOT USE THE VIDEO

## SESSION FOUR

**I'll make a brief summary of what's in chapter 4, working from the Leader's Guide. It's about listening, and I suppose one of the main things that comes out of the chapter is the great power we have to give our children a sense of being understood. Parents of teenagers often wonder what they can do with their children, but almost all teenagers will tell you, "My parents do not listen to me." Maybe that's where we need to begin if we want to influence our children, no matter what age they are.**

**The chapter introduces us to a special way of listening called *active* listening, though this is more for times when a child has *strong* feelings. The idea is a bit like holding a mirror in front of children - to listen for what they're feeling and reflect that back to them in your own words. That can help them to clarify for themselves what's going on inside them and can help them to make their own decisions and begin to manage their own problems.**

**Table 4 is a kind of summary of these ideas. If you'd like to look at it, you'll see some examples of what we mean... Maybe we'll just take a minute or two to read down through it, and if you'd like to make any comments, feel free to do so.**

Allow time for reading the page and then ask:

**Any comments on that Table, or can you see how any of these ideas might apply in your own family...?**

Move on fairly quickly to the Case Studies.


## SESSION FIVE

**I'll make a brief summary of what's in chapter 5, working from the Leader's Guide. It's about managing problems. Last week we saw how we can help our children deal with their problems just by listening to them. But there are also problems that don't just disappear with listening, so what *problem-management* skills can we use here? In the chapter we see that it's important to decide first who *owns* a problem - me or my child. If the *child* owns the problem we can use last week's skill of active listening. But if *I* own the problem, the suggestion is that I give an "I" message, i.e. I use the word "I" or**

**"me" to tell the child how I feel about the problem behaviour. That will not always work, but at least it shows respect for myself and for the child.**

**For more serious problems, there are four stages to managing problems - you can see them in section five in the section *When the child owns the problem.* Number 1, you begin with listening; number 2, you work along with the child to think up possible solutions; number 3, you help your child choose one solution that might work; and, number 4, you can fix a time to come together again to check out how the plan is working out.**

**Table 4 is a kind of summary of some of these ideas, so we'll take a minute or two to read down through it, and if you'd like to make any comments, feel free to do so.**

Allow time for reading the page and then ask any of the following questions to start the discussion:

**Any comments on that Table, or on the idea of giving - *I* messages...? Is there anything new, or anything you've learnt from the Table...? Can you see how any of these ideas might apply to you or how you could apply them yourself in your own family...?**

Move on fairly quickly to the Case Studies.


SESSION SIX

**Chapter Six looks at discipline. It suggests that, instead of telling children what to do and insisting that they do it, nagging at them or standing over them, it often helps to offer a choice and allow children to learn from the consequences of what they choose. There are lots of examples in Table 6, if you'd like to take a minute or so to read down through them...**

Allow time for reading the page. Then ask:

**Any comments on the Table, or can you see how any of these ideas might apply in your family...?**

Move on fairly quickly to the Case Studies.

## SESSION SEVEN

**Chapter seven looks at family meetings. The idea is to have a regular sit-down session with at least one child to talk through the decisions that affect that child - chores, pocket money, bedtimes, outings, anything you or they want to talk about. It's not an easier way to be a parent. It's easier to say "yes" or "no" and make the decisions yourself. But otherwise how will children learn to be responsible and to form their own values?**

**Family meetings also offer opportunities to practise all the skills taught on this programme - active listening, giving "I" messages, giving responsibility, encouraging, brainstorming, applying consequences and generally improving the level of communication in the family. With regular family meetings, children <u>also</u> grow in their ability to use these skills, and they learn many essential life skills like managing problems and handling conflict. We saw in chapter seven that family meetings may be the key to the long-term success of this programme, long after a course finishes.**

**The thinking behind this programme is that parents are the natural leaders in the home. In the last analysis, both legally and morally, you have to make the decisions, but all the time involving the children more and more in the making of decisions that affect themselves. The family meeting is a helpful way of encouraging that to happen. So let's get a clearer idea of the stages of a family meeting by looking at Table 7.**

Allow time for reading the Table. Then ask:

**Any comments on the Table, or what's your reaction to the idea of Family Meetings...?**

Move on fairly quickly to the Case Studies.


## SESSION EIGHT

**Chapter eight attempts to tie together all the different skills we've been learning. To be effective, we see that it's good to stop and ask a few questions like: "What is Jean really looking for? - attention, power, revenge, etc." or "Whose problem is this - mine or the child's?" or "How can I encourage Colin to become more responsible**

for himself in this situation?" Answering these questions will often give you a clue as to which approach to take - to back off, or listen, or encourage, or give a choice, or whatever.

What is also encouraging is that these skills can be applied to other adults, to a partner, a parent, an in-law, a neighbour, etc. The Case Studies will give you a chance to see how this can happen, so perhaps we can move directly into the case studies, since we've already looked at Table 8...

# APPENDIX 2A: AN OPTIONAL CHRISTIAN DIMENSION

*The purpose of the following pieces (most written by Flor McCarthy) is to introduce a note of calm and reflection and add a religious dimension to each session - at the same time reinforcing a central idea from the session. They can be introduced after the short relaxation and visualisation exercise towards the end of the session. The sections that are in bold are read.*

## SESSION ONE

Continue to play the music softly. (The following passage is reproduced by kind permission of "Reality" magazine.)

**You can continue to relax now, perhaps keeping your eyes closed, as you listen to a child speaking...**

**Don't spoil me. I know quite well I ought not to have all I ask for. I'm only testing you.**

**Don't be afraid to be firm with me. I prefer it. It makes me feel more secure.**

**Don't let me form bad habits. I need you to detect them at an early stage.**

**Don't correct me in front of people if you can help it. I'll take more notice if you talk quietly with me in private.**

**Don't make me feel my mistakes are sins. It upsets my sense of values.**

**Don't protect me from consequences. I need to learn the painful way sometimes.**

**Don't be too upset when I say 'I hate you.' I say it when I hate myself.**

**Don't take too much notice of my small ailments. Sometimes they get the attention I need.**

**Don't nag. If you do, I'll have to protect myself by appearing deaf.**

**Don't forget that I can't explain myself as well as I'd like to. That's why I'm not always very accurate.**

**Don't make rash promises. I feel let down when promises are broken.**

**Don't tax my honesty too much. I'm easily frightened into telling lies.**

**Don't tell me my fears are silly. They're terribly real - and you can help if you try to understand.**

**Don't put me off when I ask questions. If you do, you'll find that I stop asking and seek my information elsewhere.**

**Don't ever think it's beneath your dignity to apologise to me. An honest apology makes me feel surprisingly warm towards you.**

**Don't ever suggest that you're perfect or infallible. It gives me too great a shock when I discover you're neither.**

**Don't forget I love experimenting. I couldn't get on without it. Please put up with it.**

**Don't forget I can't thrive without lots of understanding love.** (brief pause)

**And we'll end by turning to God who is parent to all of us and who is very interested in helping us improve our parenting skills. Let's join together in praying the Lords' prayer.**

**Our Father...**

## SESSION TWO

**Some day when my children are old enough to understand, I will tell them:**

**I loved you enough to ask you about where you were going, with whom and what time you would get home.**

**I loved you enough to make you return a Mars bar - with a bite out of it - and to confess: "I stole this."**

**I loved you enough to let you see hurt, disappointment, disgust and tears in my eyes.**

**I loved you enough to admit I was wrong and ask for your forgiveness.**

**I loved you enough to let you stumble, fall, and hurt.**

**I loved you enough to give you increasing responsibility for household chores and to train you to do them well.**

**But most of all, I loved you enough to say NO when you hated me for it - that was hard for me.** (Anonymous)

**Let's join together now to pray the Lords' prayer. Our Father...**

## SESSION THREE

We live in a world that is obsessed with success. Prizes are given, not for trying but for succeeding. The unsuccessful always go away empty-handed. Those magic words "congratulations!" or "well done!" are never said to those who most need to hear them, namely, those who have tried their best but failed.

A vixen had three cubs. Once she got ill and had to send the cubs out at night in search of food. She told them to split up and to avoid the south, for the town lay in that direction. "Be careful!" she warned them. "Remember that a fox has to be very cunning."

The first cub was strong but lazy. He chose the easiest route, going westwards over flat fields. He had only gone a short distance when he entered a field that was stirring with rabbits. He grabbed a fine fat one, killed and ate it at once. When the rabbits came out again, he grabbed another and made off home with it, feeling well pleased with himself. He was back home in half an hour, without as much as a scratch on him.

"Well done" said the mother. "You're a very good cub."
And she gave him a lick of her tongue on the side of his face.

The second cub was very clever. He headed eastwards across gently rolling fields. Seeing the lights of a farmhouse ahead, he came upon a fowl yard. Amazingly there was no guard dog on duty. He quickly killed two young geese and dragged them away with him. When he was a safe distance away, he ate half of one of the geese, carefully hiding the other half. As he set out for home with the other goose, he was feeling on top of the world. He was home within an hour.

On seeing the goose the mother exclaimed, "Congratulations! You're a wonderful cub." And she gave him two licks of her tongue on the side of his face.

The third cub was small and weak. He had no choice but to head northwards into the hills. Here farmhouses were few and far between, and all were guarded by savage dogs. At one farm a dog tore his face through a wire fence. At another an angry farmer grazed him with a blast from a shotgun.

He travelled all night but caught nothing. As dawn was breaking he headed for home, exhausted, hungry and down in the dumps. On the way home he found a dead sparrow. He was about to swallow it when he thought, "I'll take it home to my mother. It's not much, but it's the best I can do." He arrived back covered in mud, a mass of bruises and cuts.

"What kept you so long?" asked the mother sharply.

"I ran into a lot of trouble," he answered feebly.

"Didn't I warn you to be careful? And what have you brought me back at the end of it all?"

With that he produced the sparrow.

"Is that all you've brought me? One of your brothers brought me a goose. The other brought me a rabbit. And this is the best you can do. You'll grow up to be a waster. Take it away and get out of my sight."

With that she chased him out of the den. Then she got the breakfast ready. On the menu was goose and rabbit. She seated the strong cub on her right-hand side and the clever cub on her left-hand side. But there was no place at the banquet table for the little cub.

In one sense the mother was right. Judged by results the little cub had come a long way behind the other two. But in another sense she was completely wrong. Judged not by results, but by the effort made and the spirit shown, the little cub had come a long, long way ahead of the other two.

God never judges us by results. To God it is the heart that matters. Criticism and encouragement go straight to the heart. Criticism closes the heart, whereas encouragement opens it.

And anything that encourages our children to open their hearts helps them to live more fully.

Let's end with the Lords' prayer said in common.

Our Father...

## SESSION FOUR

Christ came to the home of Martha and Mary. He was in the mood to talk. He was totally at their disposal. They had a marvellous opportunity to listen to him. And what happened? Martha immediately started to prepare a meal for him. Mary, however, sat down at his feet. In choosing to listen to him Christ said that Mary had chosen "the better part," that is, the more important part.

Listening is an important part of being a life-giving encouraging parent. But we could listen a great deal and understand nothing - it is only with the heart that we can listen and understand.

Christ touched the ears of those who were deaf and enabled them to hear. We need to ask him to touch our ears too because even though we may be blessed with two perfectly good ears it doesn't automatically follow that we are good listeners. (Pause).

Lord, You made the deaf hear. Touch our ears so that we may be able to listen to our children and to one another. Touch our hearts so that we may be able to understand what we hear. And help us to take time to listen to you who alone have the words of eternal life. We ask this through Christ our Lord. Amen. (brief pause)

I would like to invite you to touch one another's ears while saying the words: "May the Lord touch your ears and help you to listen with your heart."

Allow time for this. Then:

Let's end by praying the Lords' prayer in common....

## SESSION FIVE

Can you imagine how Joseph and Mary felt when they couldn't find their l2-year-old son in a big city? It hurts to care about anyone, but it hurts especially to care about our children when they begin to go their own way and to do things their way. Our peaceful world is turned upside down, as it was for Joseph and Mary. We can feel so torn and anxious when a problem arises with one of our children that the last thing we want to do is to listen. Sometimes we accuse instead of listening, instead of stopping to hear the child's point of view. Yet

**Mary's first comment was not an accusation but a question: "Son, why have you done this to us?"** (Brief pause...)

We can learn something else from the story. It is interesting that this serious problem arose when Mary and Joseph were practising their faith - on a long, tough pilgrimage to the temple in Jerusalem. Jesus grew up in a family where faith was lived - it is not surprising that they found him eventually in the temple, for he had learned to love the things of God from parents who loved them. The story has a happy ending. St. Luke says: "Jesus went down with them to Nazareth and lived under their authority... and he increased in wisdom, in stature, and in favour with God and men."

Thus, in spite of the pain it had caused, the incident had the effect of bringing them closer together as a family. They each learned something from it. Jesus came to appreciate how much Mary and Joseph cared about him, so he willingly obeyed them. And Mary and Joseph began to realise what a special child Jesus was, so they gave him scope to grow, even though it meant that he was growing from them. As so often happens, a serious problem had become a blessing. (Brief pause.)

Dear God, thank you for our children and for the problems and tensions we have with them that offer us so many opportunities to grow. We need courage, patience, wisdom and understanding in dealing with these problems. We pray for these virtues so that we may help our children grow in wisdom, in stature, and in favour with you and with others.

Perhaps we could all link hands as we recite the Lords' prayer in common...

## SESSION SIX:

Children need discipline if they are to grow properly and develop fully. By discipline is not meant the rod, but rather a loving, supportive presence in their lives. They need a close relationship with another human being that will give them a feeling of stability and security.

One day, a small, delicate tree was taken from a nursery and planted out in a public park. At first the little tree felt very lonely and deeply insecure. If left to itself, it would be at the mercy of the wind and would end up stunted and twisted out of shape.

But it was not left to itself. The caretaker came along and drove a strong, sturdy stake into the ground beside the little tree. When he was sure that the stake was rock-solid, he tied the tree to it. Suddenly the tree felt secure. It had something to cling to when the wind threatened to bend it out of shape or break it. Thanks to the stake, it began to take root in the ground. At the same time it started to put out shoots and grow upwards and outwards.

Naturally, as it grew, it began to experience a longing for independence and resented being tied to the stake. It longed to be grown up and free like the big trees it saw all around it. At times it wanted nothing else but to yield itself to the wind, and it kicked against the stake. At such times the stake had to take quite a buffeting. But it held firm.

As the tree's trunk developed, the caretaker came around and loosened the tie, thus allowing the tree room for expansion. Then one day, he came along and removed the stake altogether, and the tree was on its own. But by now it had sent down deep roots and it was straight. It had nothing to fear. It was well able to stand on its own. It was well on its way to becoming a fully-grown tree.

As I'm sure you've guessed, the tree stands for the child, the stake stands for the parents and the tie for discipline. The goal of all our discipline is to help them one day to be self-disciplined, that is, to be able to stand on their own feet. So as soon as they are capable of reasoning we can begin to explain to them the reasoning behind our rules, and we can begin to bring them into the making of decisions that concern them.

There is another dimension to all this. Children learn how God cares for them when they experience how a parent cares for them. They learn that God is always there, supporting them and gently challenging them through crises and difficulties as they experience how a parent is there beside them, supporting them in facing life's challenges. God parents us by giving us the freedom to make our own decisions and allowing us to live with the consequences, while at the same time loving and supporting us in more ways than we can imagine.

It's a tough task, and parents need each other's support. So maybe we could just give one another some sign of support now - anything you like to show your willingness to support and encourage each other... (brief pause)

Dear God, thank you for our children and for the opportunities you give us to strengthen them and help them to grow. We ask you to strengthen us parents for we are often weak before the cold winds of life. Help us to know when to be strong and firm, and when to be gentle and yielding, so that we may be able to offer our children a supportive and reliable presence. And grant that they may know your love and support through our love and support. We make our prayer through Christ our Lord. Amen.

## SESSION SEVEN:

There is something beautiful about every child, even though she or he is unfinished. They are so full of energy, so alive, so inquisitive before the mystery of life. They have a habit of asking all the important questions... Questions about life, about death, about God. They want to know why they are alive. They want to know where the mysterious journey of life is leading. This mysterious journey that every one of us is making.

Our children's journey has begun. As yet, they may merely be playing on the shore of life. All the ocean of adult life stretches out before them, with its challenges and dangers. It is our job to gradually introduce them to the ocean. We do this though we know one day they will hoist a sail, put out to sea and disappear over the horizon.

"Though your children come through you," Kahlil Gibran says, "they do not come from you. You are merely the bows from which your children are shot forth as living arrows. And while you may provide a house for their bodies, you cannot provide a house for their souls."

It is from God that we come when we land on the shore of life. It is to him we return when life's voyage is ended. (pause.)

And we will have done our job if we have given our children a map, a compass and bread for the journey. We can begin now by gradually giving them a greater say in the decisions that affect their lives. The family meeting is a most helpful tool for encouraging that. We leave it to God to bring them safely to the eternal port.

Dear God, our children have come from you, they belong to you and it is to you that we want them to return. Thank you for the privilege of caring for them during our short lifetime and help us not to forget that you're in charge, guiding them on life's journey. Help us to prepare them well for this journey and to gradually give them more and more say in the decisions that affect their lives, and lead them eventually into the fullness of your kingdom. Through Christ Our Lord. Amen.

## SESSION EIGHT:
In bringing up children we have to be prepared for disappointments.
Read Matthew 13: 24-30

How do you think that farmer felt when he saw weeds growing among his wheat? He felt angry. He felt bitterly disappointed. It seemed as if all his work was wasted.

But he eventually calmed down and was able to see things in a balanced way. So what if there were some weeds in his field! There was wheat there too, wheat that was as green and vibrant as ever. He would have to work harder at encouraging the wheat in the hope that it would outgrow the weeds. Even if the harvest fell short of the hundred per cent he had been hoping for, he was confident that it would still be adequate for his needs.

What then if we find there are weeds growing in that little family plot on which we lavish so much time and care? In other words, our children are causing problems or in trouble. We may feel angry and let down. How can those children for whom we sacrificed so much repay us in this way? We may look for someone or something to blame - companions, television... We may even blame ourselves, feeling that we have failed them.

But we've got to have a realistic view of things. Our children are not lumps of clay to be moulded into the exact shapes we design for them. They are individuals with minds and wills of their own. Besides, evil exists. Let us not be so foolish as to believe that we can shelter our children from it forever.

We can take heart from the example of Christ. He knew what it was like to be disappointed by people. Among the twelve apostles there was one who denied him (Peter) and another who betrayed him (Judas). Even in the garden which he himself had tended so carefully for three long years, the weeds still grew. Yet he didn't write the garden off. He still believed in it and worked on it. And, in spite of setbacks, in time it produced a harvest that the world is still reaping.

There are powerful forces working against us. But our faith assures us that God is working with us, wanting the best for us and for our children. So let's keep a sense of balance - and a sense of humour. We can afford to.

In any case, the field isn't ours. It belongs to God. And though we planted the crop, it is God who will reap the harvest.

What harvest can we expect anyway? Not worldly success, certainly, but goodness. God wants our children to become responsible, co-operative and loving adults. That is the "wheat" which at the harvest time of life will be gathered into our heavenly Father's barn. (brief pause)

Dear God, Yours is the seed and yours is the harvest. Thank you for giving us the opportunity to play our part in tending the crop. We offer our children to you just as they are, weeds as well as wheat. Help us to keep a sense of balance and to remember that the success of the harvest does not depend on us. For yours is the seed and yours is the harvest. In Christ Jesus our Lord.

# APPENDIX 2B: ISLAMIC DIMENSION (OPTIONAL)

*The Islamic dimension below has been prepared by Dr Mamoun Mobayed for use by Muslim parenting groups.*


## SESSION ONE:

I want to ask you now to relax and make yourselves comfortable as you listen to a reflection:

"Don't spoil me...    ...of understanding love. (See Reflection 1 in Appendix 2A)

Maybe we'll just end by turning to God who is the Rab for all of us, and who is very interested in helping us improving our parenting skills.

So let's join together in a short prayer to Allah.  O Allah...


## SESSION TWO:

Please relax and make yourselves comfortable, and let us turn our hearts and minds to Allah.

Some day when my children are old enough to understand...
...that was hard for me. (See Reflection 2 in Appendix 2A))

Let us join together now to pray to Allah.  O Allah.


## SESSION THREE:

Please relax now, as you listen to the reflection. We live in a world...
...to live more fully. (See Reflection 3 in Appendix 2A)

Let us end with a short prayer to our Lord.  O Allah...


## SESSION FOUR:

Please relax now as you listen to the reflection.

Listening is a very important part of being a life-giving encouraging parent. But we could listen a great deal and understand nothing - it is only with the heart that we can listen and understand.

# APPENDIX 2A: OPTIONAL ISLAMIC DIMENSION

O Allah, You make the deaf hear. Help us so that we may be able to listen to our children, and to one another. O Allah, change our hearts so that we may be able to understand what we hear. And help us to take time to listen to you who alone have the words of eternal life. Amen.

## SESSION FIVE:

Please relax now as we pray together:

O Allah, Lord of the universe, thank you for our children and the problems and tensions we have with them that offer us so many opportunities to grow. We need courage, patience, wisdom and understanding in dealing with these problems. We pray for these virtues so that we may help our children grow in wisdom, in stature, and in favour with you and with others.

## SESSION SIX:

Please relax now as you listen to the reflection.

Children need discipline if they...    ...each other. (See Reflection 6 in Appendix 2A)

Dear God, thank you for our children and for the opportunities you give us to strengthen them and help them to grow. We ask you to strengthen us parents for we are often weak before the cold winds of life. Help us to know when to be strong and firm, and when to be gentle and yielding, so that we may be able to offer our children a supportive and reliable presence. And grant that they may know your love and support. O Allah, it is you we ask. Amen.

## SESSION SEVEN:

Please relax now as you listen to the reflection:

There is something beautiful about every child...    ...to the eternal port. (See Reflection 7 in Appendix 2A)

Dear God, Our children have come from you, they belong to you and it is to you that we want them to return. Thank you for the privilege of caring for them during our short lifetime and help us not to forget that you're in charge, guiding them on life's journey. Help us to prepare them well for this journey and gradually to give them more and more say in the decisions that affect their lives. And lead them eventually into the fullness of your Paradise. Amen.


SESSION EIGHT:

Please relax now as you listen to the reflections:

In bringing up children we have to be prepared for disappointments. What then if we find there are weeds growing in... ...which at the harvest time of life will be gathered into our Lord's barn. (See Reflection 8 in Appendix 2A)

Dear God, Yours is the seed and yours is the harvest. Thank you for giving us the opportunity to play our part in tending the crop. We offer our children to you just as they are, the weeds as well as the wheat. Help us to keep a sense of balance and to remember that the success of the harvest does not depend on us. For yours is the seed and yours is the harvest. O Allah, Lord of the universe. Amen.

## SAMPLE LETTER FROM A SCHOOL

Dear Parents,

I am conscious that it can be much more difficult to bring up children today because times have changed so much. So I am pleased to let you know that the school is helping to set up a parenting programme, "What can a parent do?" which will start shortly. The programme involves one session each week for eight weeks. The sessions, which include watching a video, will be held in the (evenings) and will last two hours.

This course is for ordinary parents from every walk of life. You will be most welcome, whether you are a lone parent or a couple - but if you are a couple, we strongly encourage you to attend as a couple. The purpose of the course is to give you a chance to stand back from everything and, with the support of other parents, look at ways of improving communication with your children, disciplining them, etc. There will be great respect for different approaches and no one will be preaching at you or telling you how to bring up your children! But you will also find many practical ideas in the attractive handbook which is supplied as part of the course. The entire course will cost only £1 per session to meet basic expenses, including the cost of the book.

This is not a dull, classroom-type course. I think you will find it relaxing and enjoyable, you'll have some good laughs and you will probably make new friends. Tens of thousands of parents have experienced the course in the past year alone and are enthusiastic about the results. It has helped them to set clear guidelines and encourage effective discipline in the home. It also reduces tension, squabbling and fighting and creates a more relaxed, respectful and friendly atmosphere within the home. Many parents cannot believe the difference it makes to themselves and to their children.

If you are interested, please fill in the attached form. Those who wish to bring along a friend are welcome to do so, but please indicate the extra name on the form. When we know the number interested, we will send you further details. I hope you will be able to attend.

Yours sincerely,
(Principal)

------------------------------------------------------------------------------------------------

**REPLY FORM** - return by........ (date).

Please reserve a place for me on "What can a parent do?"

NAME(S) _____

ADDRESS _____

_____

The ad. below, posted on notice boards in health clinics, libraries, etc., has helped to advertise the parenting courses.

## CALLING ALL PARENTS - OF YOUNG CHILDREN & TEENAGERS

*I've tried everything. I don't know what else to do!*

*I feel like I'm banging my head against a brick wall*

*Why do I have to keep saying the same things over and over again?*

*There's got to be a better way to bring up children!*

Do some of these remarks sound familiar? Would you like to join the hundreds of thousands of parents who have enjoyed an EFFECTIVE PARENTING course in the past few years? The purpose of the course is to help parents find their *own* ways of enjoying their children more and being more effective. You will find it a relaxing, enjoyable experience; you'll have some laughs and you'll make new friends. Courses start again soon. (Daytime with Crèche, and Evenings)

CONTACT: